Eyewitness
VIETNAM WAR

Vietminh medal
for bravery

VC guerrillas
demonstrate ambush

Soviet-made 7D
grenade launcher

U.S. lensatic
military compass

U.S. military
dog tags

Peace-symbol
button

PENICILLIN
500000单位

Montagnard
crossbow and
arrows

Chinese-made
penicillin, used by
the Viet Cong

USS *Maddox* uniform patch

Eyewitness
VIETNAM WAR

Written by
STUART MURRAY

DK Publishing, Inc.

Lyndon B.
Johnson 1964
campaign button

North Vietnamese Air
Force symbol

M-1 bayonet

LONDON, NEW YORK, MELBOURNE,
MUNICH, and DELHI

DK Publishing, Inc.
Senior Editor Barbara Berger
Senior Designer Tai Blanche
Additional Design Jeremy Canceko,
Jee Chang, and Jessica Lasher
Assistant Managing Art Editor Michelle Baxter
Creative Director Tina Vaughan
Jacket Art Director Dirk Kaufman
Production Manager Ivor Parker
DTP Coordinator Milos Orlovic

Media Projects, Inc.
Executive Editor Carter Smith
Project Editor Aaron R. Murray
Associate Editor Margaret C.F. McLaughlin
Production Manager James A. Burmester
Consultants Clifford J. Rogers and Steve R. Waddell,
United States Military Academy
Cartography Ron Toelke, Rob Stokes
Picture Researcher Erika Rubel
Copy Editor Glenn Novak

This edition published in the United States in 2005
by DK Publishing, Inc.
375 Hudson Street, New York, NY 10014

05 06 07 08 09 10 9 8 7 6 5 4 3 2 1

Copyright © 2005 DK Publishing, Inc.

DK Publishing, Inc. offers special discounts for bulk purchases for sales
promotions or premiums. Specific, large-quantity needs can be met with
special editions, including personalized covers, excerpts of existing
guides, and corporate imprints. For more information, contact Special
Markets Department, DK Publishing, Inc.,
375 Hudson Street, New York, NY 10014
Fax: 646-674-4017

Library of Congress Cataloging-in-Publication Data

Murray, Stuart, 1948-
  Eyewitness Vietnam War / written by Stuart Murray.--
1st American ed.
    p. cm. -- (Eyewitness books)
  Includes index.
  ISBN 0-7566-1166-0 (plc : alk. paper) -- ISBN 0-7566-1165-2
(alb : alk. paper)
  1. Vietnamese Conflict, 1961-1975--Juvenile literature. I. Title.
II. DK eyewitness books.
  DS557.7.M85 2005
  959.704'3--dc22

                                        2004024516

Color reproduction by Colourscan, Singapore
Printed in China by Toppan Printing Co.,(Shenzhen) Ltd.

Discover more at
www.dk.com

U.S. infantry helmet

South Vietnamese
200-dong note, 1966

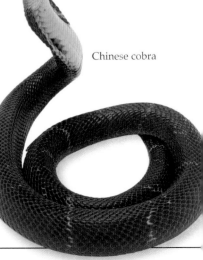

Soviet-made antitank
land mine

Chinese cobra

North
Vietnamese
stamp

PRC-9 backpack
field radio

Contents

U.S. M-16A1
assault rifle

War in French Indochina

The GLOBAL DESTRUCTION caused by World War II (1939–1945) weakened France's colonial empire. During the war, the Japanese took control of French colonies in the Indochina Peninsula of Southeast Asia. In 1945, Vietnamese nationalists took up arms to gain independence. Led by Ho Chi Minh (1890–1969), a Communist, they first battled the occupying Japanese forces.

Many fighters in Ho's nationalist army, known as the Vietminh, were trained by advisors from the United States, which was at war with Japan. After Japan's defeat, France wanted to reestablish control over Indochina, but Ho declared Vietnam's independence. He tried to negotiate with the French, but they would not recognize Vietnam. The stage was set for the First Indochina War.

EMPEROR BAO DAI
European-educated Bao Dai (1913–1997), shown above with French officials in the 1920s, was the 13th and last emperor of Vietnam. He was recognized by France as the country's ruler, but to Vietnamese nationalists he was a French puppet—they wanted an independent republic with elected rulers.

Vietnamese dragon   Bao Dai stamp

Japanese "Rising Sun" battle flag

JAPANESE WARSHIPS
Japan's battleships patrol Indochina waters as her troops on land fight the Communist-led Vietminh nationalists. Ho Chi Minh's army gained valuable military experience fighting against the Japanese.

U.S. ADVISORS TRAIN VIETMINH
An American military advisor looks on as Vietminh fighters practice throwing grenades. The Vietminh included Communist and non-communist nationalists. After the war, Ho Chi Minh won support from Communist countries—the People's Republic of China and the Soviet Union. The United States objected to Communist influence over the growing independence movements of French Indochina.

Map of Vietnam

Portrait of Ho Chi Minh

Early currency of the Democratic Republic of Vietnam (DRV)

DECLARING INDEPENDENCE

Ho Chi Minh, right, addresses Vietnamese nationalists gathered in the northern Vietnamese city of Hanoi, below, on September 2, 1945, the day of Japan's surrender. Ho declared the establishment of the independent Democratic Republic of Vietnam (DRV). At first, the French granted limited freedoms to the DRV, but clashes followed between Vietnamese government forces and French troops. As growing hostility between the DRV and France made war unavoidable, the United States backed French domination of Vietnam.

FRENCH MILITARY PARADE

Newly arrived French soldiers drive through Hanoi past cheering French colonial residents and their Vietnamese supporters. The French tried to reestablish military control in Indochina just after World War II. Some Vietnamese favored French rule and bitterly opposed the Vietminh nationalists—especially as the Vietminh became increasingly influenced by communism. Many of the French-allied Vietnamese were educated in Europe, and had converted from Buddhism to Catholicism.

TRUMAN AND ACHESON

U.S. president Harry S. Truman (1884–1972), left, meets with Secretary of State Dean Acheson (1893–1971) in the late 1940s. Both believed that if Vietnam were controlled by Ho's Communists, then other Indochinese countries also would become Communist. Acheson persuaded Truman to give France financial and military aid to oppose the Communists and the DRV.

INDOCHINA TIMELINE

1940 Japan takes over French Indochina in World War II.

1941 Ho Chi Minh establishes the Vietminh, the "League for the Independence of Vietnam."

1945 Japan surrenders. Ho Chi Minh forms the Democratic Republic of Vietnam (DRV).

1946 French colonial troops clash with DRV forces, sparking the First Indochina War (1946–1954).

1950 French suffer defeats; United States sets up the Military Assistance and Advisory Group (MAAG) to further aid France.

1951 France controls cities; Vietminh control countryside.

1954 Vietminh take Dien Pien Phu base and defeat French, ending First Indochina War. Treaty in Geneva, Switzerland, temporarily divides Vietnam into North and South, calls for vote on Vietnamese future.

France loses Indochina

EARLY IN THE FIRST INDOCHINA WAR, American military supplies and equipment gave the French an advantage over the Vietminh. The French captured the cities, but Ho Chi Minh and his top general, Vo Nguyen Giap (b. 1912), were unwilling to accept defeat. They reorganized their army in the jungles and mountains and received aid from Communist China. The war went on for years. In late 1953, the French built a new base at Dien Bien Phu, in the northern mountains. By the spring, Colonel Christian de Castries and 15,000 troops were surrounded there by Giap's 55,000 men and hundreds of artillery pieces. After a 55-day siege, De Castries surrendered in May 1954. The victorious Vietminh prepared for an independent Vietnam.

Canteen

FACING IMPOSSIBLE ODDS
In a bunker at Dien Bien Phu, Colonel De Castries (1902–1991) faces surrender or death. His force was completely cut off from help and under heavy bombardment by Vietminh artillery. De Castries was taken prisoner, but survived captivity and returned home.

Sandbags protect walls

ASSAULT FROM THE AIR
French paratroopers land at Dien Bien Phu in late 1953 to establish a new base. By next spring, Vietminh artillery had destroyed the French airfield, and ground attacks were capturing French positions one by one. The whole world watched the battle raging at Dien Bien Phu.

U.S. military gear used by French

PLANNING A FRENCH DEFEAT
Vietminh leader Ho Chi Minh, left, studies the layout of besieged Dien Bien Phu, a French base in the mountains on the Vietnam-Laos border. Along with Ho is General Vo Nguyen Giap, right, who commanded Vietminh forces in the battle. Although the French won several major clashes during the war, in the end Giap and Ho outgeneraled them.

Soldier's bundled bedding and coat

DOOMED FRENCH DEFENDERS
After fighting bravely for almost two months, these weary French troops wait for the end to come. They had not expected the Vietminh to drag cannon into the mountains and bombard their base. Approximately 2,000 French troops and 8,000 Vietminh died in the campaign, with 10,800 French captured. Most of the captives died of hunger and disease.

FRENCH HEADQUARTERS BUNKER FALLS
Victorious Vietnamese fighters raise their red and gold flag over Colonel De Castries's steel-covered bunker. This central command center fell to the Vietminh on May 7, 1954, after a siege of 55 days. One soldier waves the flag while two others stand guard. Seven weeks later, a veteran French armored battalion, Groupement Mobile (G.M.) 100, was ambushed on the road and almost completely destroyed by the Vietminh. This decisive defeat, combined with the fall of Dien Bien Phu, ended the First Indochina War.

Communist flag

The Geneva Accords

Peace terms ending the First Indochina War were signed in Geneva, Switzerland, by the French and the Vietminh, on July 20, 1954. Known as the Geneva Accords, they gave the Communists control of Vietnam north of the 17th parallel. A non-communist government ruled South Vietnam. The Vietnamese were to hold elections within two years to decide on their form of government. The United States opposed a Communist-led Vietnam, however, and refused to accept the accords or an election.

Rubble from artillery bombardment

General Henri Delteil

North Vietnam

17th parallel

South Vietnam

Value of stamp

Communist star

INDOCHINA TRUCE SIGNING
Former French general Henri Delteil signs truce documents on July 20, 1954, ending Indochina hostilities. A European official and Vietnamese delegates look on during the ceremony in Geneva's Palace of Nations. Month-long negotiations were held in the palace before the signing.

DIVIDED VIETNAM
This North Vietnamese stamp shows Vietnam separated into North and South by a line at the 17th parallel. The South China Sea is blue, at right, and Communist China is north. The former French colonies of Laos and Cambodia are to the left. They became independent in the mid-1950s.

Vietminh medal for bravery

VICTORY PARADE
Triumphant Vietminh troops driving military trucks through Hanoi in October 1954 are cheered on by crowds lining the city streets. French colonial forces had recently pulled out of Hanoi and departed for South Vietnam. After almost eight years of war this northern city was now under the complete control of Vietminh forces. Hanoi became North Vietnam's capital.

DIEN BIEN PHU TO ARMISTICE

- **1953** 90,000 French troops in Vietnam, with 100,000 Vietnamese National Army (colonial) troops; Vietminh forces number 200,000.
- **November 1953** French build base at Dien Bien Phu.
- **December 1953** French troops assemble at Dien Bien Phu, prepare for major battle.
- **February 1954** Giap surrounds Dien Bien Phu.
- **March 13, 1954** Vietminh start ground assaults.
- **May 1, 1954** Final ground attacks begin.
- **May 7, 1954** Dien Bien Phu falls.
- **June 24–July 17, 1954** G.M. 100, a 3,000-strong armored unit, wiped out.
- **August 1, 1954** Armistice ends the First Indochina War.

U.S. advisors in Vietnam

The "Advisory Phase" began in 1955, as President Dwight D. Eisenhower (1890–1969) sent hundreds of military advisors to aid the Republic of (South) Vietnam (RVN). The Eisenhower administration wanted to prevent the spread of communism in Southeast Asia. It helped anti-communist Ngo Dinh Diem (1901–1963) take power in a corrupt election that year. Thousands of angry South Vietnamese armed to fight Diem's government. Diem called them "Viet Cong" (VC), meaning Vietnamese Communists. These anti-Diem forces were led by the National Liberation Front (NLF), an alliance of political groups. The NLF was headquartered in the North, while VC guerrillas fought in the South. When John F. Kennedy (1917–1963) became U.S. president in 1961, he increased American involvement. In late 1963, Diem was overthrown and killed, and Kennedy was assassinated.

IN FLIGHT
Refugees from northern Vietnam rush southward in 1954 to escape Hanoi's new Communist government. Other Vietnamese, favoring communism, chose to move north.

FIRST PRESIDENT OF SOUTH VIETNAM
Diem speaks at his 1955 inauguration. He removed Emperor Bao Dai as head of state and punished political opponents. A Roman Catholic, Diem favored members of his own religion even though the nation was 80 percent Buddhist.

Grenade launcher

U.S. Army-issue helmet

IN JUNGLE WATERS
U.S. military advisors and troops from the Army of the Republic of Vietnam (ARVN) keep gear dry as they cross a muddy river in 1963. More than 14,000 U.S. military advisors were serving in Vietnam by then.

South Vietnamese 200-dong note, 1966

19th-century Vietnamese hero Nguyen Hué

Sacks of personal possessions

AN ANGRY PROTEST
Buddhists struggle with police in Saigon during a demonstration against Diem's government in 1963. The protesters objected to persecution of their faith and called for peaceful negotiations with the Communists. Diem also was opposed by ARVN and U.S. military leaders, who felt he was ineffective in destroying the VC.

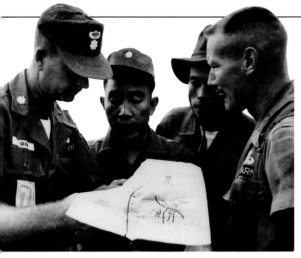

President Kennedy gives a press conference on the threat of Communist power in Southeast Asia in 1961. During his presidency, more than $500 million in U.S. military aid flowed each year to South Vietnam. JFK's administration disliked Diem's corrupt government. The United States did not publicly object when ARVN generals executed Diem on November 1, 1963.

Laos

Communist-controlled regions of Laos are shaded

REVIEWING A BATTLE PLAN

Colonel John Paul Vann (1924–1972), left, examines a map with ARVN and U.S. officers. Vann was a key figure in MAAG—the U.S. Military Assistance and Advisory Group, which oversaw the advisors in Vietnam. He objected to the careless use of heavy firepower. He preferred winning the loyalty of the people, and publicly spoke out for more effective South Vietnamese leadership.

MAAG uniform patch

CONSPIRATORS AGAINST DIEM

Ambitious ARVN generals led by Duong Van Minh, near right, murdered President Diem in November 1963 and took over the government. These men were soon overthrown by other generals eager to rule South Vietnam. As U.S. involvement escalated (increased) the republic was rocked by military coups (overthrows).

JFK's limousine

CHICAGO DAILY NEWS

PRESIDENT IS KILLED

Texas Sniper Escapes; Johnson Sworn In

Story Begins on Next Page

Chicago Daily News front page coverage of JFK's assasination

KENNEDY'S ASSASSINATION

President Kennedy and first lady Jacqueline Kennedy were riding in a motorcade through Dallas on November 22, 1963, when he was shot by a sniper. Vice President Lyndon B. Johnson, below, took the oath of office with Mrs. Kennedy at his side. Historians disagree over whether JFK would have escalated U.S. involvement in Vietnam—which LBJ did.

THE MAIN PLAYERS

- **ARVN** Army of the Republic of (South) Vietnam; rose from Vietnamese National Army (former French allies).
- **RVN** Republic of (South) Vietnam.
- **DRV** Democratic Republic of (North) Vietnam.
- **NLF** National Liberation Front, organized by Ho in 1960.
- **MAAG** Military Assistance and Advisory Group, formed by U.S. in 1950 to aid France in Indochina. Replaced by **MACV** (Military Assistance Command, Vietnam) in 1962.

Gulf of Tonkin Incident

IN THE SUMMER OF 1964, the U.S. destroyer *Maddox* was operating in the Gulf of Tonkin, close to North Vietnam. She was conducting electronic surveillance (gathering information) for secret ARVN and U.S. raids on North Vietnamese naval bases. On August 2, the *Maddox* was fired on by torpedo boats challenging her presence in North Vietnamese waters. The *Maddox* returned fire and called in air support. One torpedo boat was sunk, and the others escaped. *Maddox* commander Herbert L. Ogier's report went directly to President Johnson. Two nights later, Ogier's electronics operators thought another attack was developing. The ship fired into the darkness and maneuvered against torpedoes that seemed to be heading its way. LBJ now ordered airstrikes on North Vietnamese coastal installations. On August 7, Congress passed the Gulf of Tonkin Resolution, giving him broad war powers. Although it became clear the *Maddox* crew had been mistaken about the second attack, LBJ's course was set. He committed the United States to waging war against Vietnamese Communists.

★ North Vietnamese cities attacked by U.S. airstrikes
★ U.S. ship attacked by NVA patrol boats
▬ U.S. air attacks

GULF OF TONKIN
The 1964 torpedo-boat attack on the *Maddox* was an attempt to drive away U.S. warships supporting secret assaults on North Vietnamese naval bases. The incident, in the Gulf of Tonkin, sparked airstrikes by the United States.

Destroyer insignia

USS Maddox jacket patch

THE TONKIN CLASH
The USS *Maddox* engages North Vietnamese torpedo boats in the Gulf of Tonkin on August 2, 1964. The *Maddox* was a World War II-era destroyer that had been modernized for electronic surveillance. She was attacked while stationed four miles (6 km) off an island base for North Vietnamese patrol boats. The U.S. Navy claimed these were international waters, saying the *Maddox* had a right to be there.

Shell from Maddox *falling into water*

USS MADDOX OFFICERS
Captain John J. Herrick, far left, headed a destroyer unit that included the *Maddox.*The warship's commanding officer was Herbert Ogier, right. The unit was part of a naval operation called "Desoto Patrol," which observed North Vietnamese naval movements.

TORPEDO BOAT UNDER FIRE
This photograph taken from the *Maddox* shows a North Vietnamese motor torpedo boat dashing across the horizon. Shells from the warship crash down close by. Three high-speed boats launched several torpedoes at the *Maddox*, which had to maneuver to avoid them. The warship's guns damaged all three boats. Warplanes from the carrier USS *Ticonderoga* | soon joined the fight. One torpedo boat was destroyed, but the other two sped away, ending the engagement.

North Vietnamese torpedo boat

U.S. F-8 Crusader jet

AIR CAMPAIGN BEGINS

A U.S. warplane roars from the deck of the aircraft carrier USS *Constellation* in August 1964. Bombers struck North Vietnamese naval bases in the Gulf of Tonkin. In spring 1965, the air attacks expanded into Operation Rolling Thunder, the bombing of North Vietnam's supply routes and munitions storage areas (see pages 20–21). This three-year campaign was interrupted several times as LBJ attempted unsuccessfully to make the Communists negotiate.

The deck of a carrier was twice the size of a football field

McNAMARA DEFENDS WAR

U.S. defense secretary Robert S. McNamara (b. 1916) points to a map showing the Gulf of Tonkin. McNamara is explaining the *Maddox* clash to the Washington press corps on August 4, 1964. The attack was termed the "Gulf of Tonkin Incident." McNamara announced the United States was now "moving substantial military reinforcements" to Southeast Asia.

NAVY AND MARINE CORPS MEDAL

This medal is awarded to Navy personnel for heroism in noncombat situations. Naval duties are often dangerous, especially at sea, and can require outstanding acts of courage.

North Vietnamese torpedo boat

Maddox's cannon fires on torpedo boats

U.S. M-14 rifle

"Americanization" of the conflict

Although there was no formal declaration of war, President Johnson fully used the war powers of the Gulf of Tonkin Resolution. He committed the U.S. military to Vietnam in a policy known as the "Americanization" of the war. He hoped U.S. military strength would persuade the Communists to accept the South Vietnamese government. In addition to the Rolling Thunder air campaign, LBJ now sent troops to South Vietnam to protect U.S. military installations. The first Marines arrived by landing craft on beaches near Da Nang in March 1965. Soldiers soon were in action against the Viet Cong. This first large-scale American military involvement marked the end of the advisory period in Vietnam.

The Americanization phase of the Second Indochina War—better known as the Vietnam War—war had begun. By July 1965 more than 50,000 U.S. troops were in South Vietnam.

MARINES HIT THE BEACH

Marines splash ashore near Da Nang, South Vietnam, on March 18, 1965. They are heading for an airfield they have been assigned to protect against VC attacks. Additional U.S. forces were arriving at other places, and American television showed many of these events. This was the first military conflict to be seen on television.

Communist and U.S. allies

ALLIES WERE IMPORTANT TO THE U.S. and South Vietnamese war effort, but they were even more crucial to the Communists. The United States and South Vietnam could have waged war without Allied support, but the Vietnamese Communists did not have the industrial might to arm the troops they needed. North Vietnam and the Viet Cong received military supplies and financial aid from Communist China and the Soviet Union. American and RVN forces were supported by the "Free World Forces": troops from South Korea and nations in the Southeast Asia Treaty Organization (SEATO). South Korea sent the most troops to Vietnam—312,000. Australia was next, with 47,000. The Philippines, Thailand, and New Zealand also contributed troops to fight against the Communists.

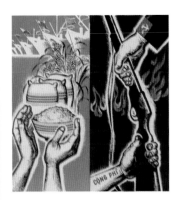

ALLIED PROPAGANDA
In this South Vietnamese poster, Allied nations are represented by flags on the top left. They offer bags of grain and a bowl of rice to help the Vietnamese, while the Soviet Union, on the right, offers only guns and destruction.

CHINESE MUNITIONS
This Chinese-made 120-mm mortar round was captured at a VC supply base in Cambodia, before it could be transported to guerrillas fighting in South Vietnam.

DRV prime minister Pham Van Dong (1906–2000)

A WARM WELCOME TO CHINA
North Vietnamese Communist Party heads and government officials receive an enthusiastic greeting from the Chinese premier, Zhou En-lai, on a state visit to Beijing, the Chinese capital, in 1973.

Vietnamese Communist Party leader Le Duan (1908–1986)

DRV (North Vietnamese) flag

Clasped hands

FRIENDS' DECORATION
The Vietnamese inscription on this medal, awarded to foreigners who aided the DRV, reads "Solidarity against American aggression."

Chinese premier Zhou En-lai (1898–1976)

SOVIET MONEY
The U.S.S.R. provided financial aid to Vietnamese Communists. Shown here is a Soviet 10-ruble note.

Portrait of Soviet premier Vladimir Ilich Lenin

Cuban Communist Party leader Blas Roca (1908–1987)

North Vietnamese president Ho Chi Minh (1890–1969)

Soviet premier Nikita Khrushchev (1894–1971)

Hungarian Party leader Janos Kadar (1912–1989)

Soviet president Leonid Brezhnev (1906–1982)

HO IN RUSSIA
Ho Chi Minh, second from left, joins Soviet officials and leaders from other Communist states to view a military parade in Moscow in 1961. The Soviets are celebrating the Russian Revolution that brought Communists to power in 1917.

RVN prime minister Nguyen Cao Ky (b. 1930)

Australian prime minister Harold Holt (1908–1967)

South Korean president Park Chung Hee (1917–1979)

Philippines president Ferdinand Marcos (1917–1989)

New Zealand prime minister Keith Holyoake (1904–1983)

RVN chief of state Nguyen Van Thieu (1923–2001)

Thai prime minister Thanom Kittikachorn (1912–2004)

U.S. president Lyndon Johnson (1908–1973)

SEATO LEADERS CONFER IN MANILA

Heads of the SEATO nations and nonmembers South Korea and South Vietnam meet in the Philippine capital, Manila, to discuss the Indochina conflict, in October 1966. SEATO was founded in September 1954 under the direction of the United States. Its purpose was to prevent more Southeast Asian countries from falling under Communist rule. SEATO's main task was to support the U.S. military presence in Vietnam. SEATO was disbanded in 1977.

FREE WORLD FORCES HANG TAG
This I.D. tag was attached to a button and worn on the shirts of troops who were termed by the allies as "Free World Forces."

PHILIPPINE AWARDS
President Marcos pins medals on Filipino soldiers being honored in Vietnam for bravery and outstanding achievements, in July 1967. He was visiting their headquarters in Tay Ninh, South Vietnam. The first Filipino troops arrived in Indochina in the summer of 1966.

Flower wreath given to welcome President Marcos

Australian service medal

AUSSIE AMBUSH
Members of the 7th Australian Royal Regiment communicate by radio while setting up an ambush in Vietnamese hill country. "Aussies" usually operated guerrilla-style. In 1966, a 101-man combat team fought off an assault by more than 2,500 VC at Long Tan.

South Korean White Horse division patch

U.S-made M-1 carbine

SOUTH KOREAN TROOPS
Above, a Korean martial arts instructor demonstrates a flying kick, in 1968. At right, Koreans stand guard over VC guerrillas just taken prisoner, c. 1966. South Koreans composed the third-largest Allied army, after the United States and South Vietnam. Koreans were among the most aggressive of the Free World Forces. They maintained three full divisions in Vietnam: White Horse, Blue Dragon, and Tiger.

The leaders

At the start of the Vietnam War, Vietnamese Communist leaders had been in power for more than 20 years. They had vast experience in military organization and guerrilla tactics. American and South Vietnamese leaders, on the other hand, were mostly politicians with little military experience. Ho Chi Minh and Vo Nguyen Giap stayed in power for most of the war, while U.S. and RVN leaders came and went. The Communists fought with all their might, but the United States had to conduct a "limited war." This meant trying to use only enough force to make the Communists stop fighting. The United States did not want to employ its great military power to destroy North Vietnam.

HO CHI MINH (1890–1969)
"Uncle Ho," as his people called him, symbolized Vietnamese patriotism. Ho's struggle against French and Japanese occupation prepared him for the Vietnam War. He died before the final Communist triumph in 1975.

NGUYEN HUU THO (1910–1996)
Tho was a French-educated lawyer who became chairman of the National Liberation Front. Imprisoned by the Ngo Dinh Diem regime, Tho escaped, and went on to lead Viet Cong guerrilla forces. After the war, Tho became vice president of Vietnam.

VO NGUYEN GIAP (b. 1912)
General Giap led Communist forces in Vietnam from the 1940s to 1972. His military career was a great success, but younger generals took over for the last years of the war. Giap retired as minister of national defense in 1980.

"We are determined to fight for independence, national unity, democracy, and peace."

**HO CHI MINH
IN A PROCLAMATION
ON MAY 8, 1954**

TRAN DO (1923–2002)
Tran Do was deputy commander of Viet Cong forces operating in South Vietnam. Do, who fought against the French, was also a general in the North Vietnamese army and a high-ranking member of the Communist Party. Years after the war, he fell out of favor with the Communist-led national government for criticizing the slow development of Vietnamese democracy.

PHAM VAN DONG (1908–2000)
In 1930, Dong helped Ho Chi Minh found the Indochinese Communist Party. He became prime minister of North Vietnam in 1950. Dong, right, walks with Cambodia's Prince Norodom Sihanouk.

NGUYEN VAN THIEU (1924–2001)
Shown voting in an election, Thieu was president of South Vietnam from 1967–1973. During the First Indochina War, he fought for the Vietminh army but then changed sides. He joined French colonial forces and later rose to power in South Vietnam. Thieu often attempted to control ARVN units in the field. This angered his generals, who had their own plans.

WILLIAM C. WESTMORELAND (b. 1914)
A veteran leader, General Westmoreland was commander of U.S. forces in Vietnam when the first American combat troops landed in 1965. He led U.S. forces in Vietnam until he was replaced by Creighton Abrams in 1968.

Lyndon B. Johnson campaign button

NGUYEN CAO KY (b. 1930)
A South Vietnamese fighter pilot and air force leader, General Ky was the premier in President Thieu's government from 1965–1971. Ky was often in the news, seen wearing flashy uniforms. When Saigon fell to the Communists in 1975, he fled to America.

LYNDON B. JOHNSON (1908–1973)
Johnson feared being the president who let Vietnam become Communist. He is seen, below right, with advisors aboard the presidential plane, Air Force One, flying back from meeting South Vietnamese leaders in Hawaii. Vice President Hubert H. Humphrey (1911–1978) sits at far left.

"We have no ambition there for ourselves, we seek no wider war."

LYNDON B. JOHNSON, FEBRUARY 17, 1965

NIXON AND KISSINGER
President Richard M. Nixon (1913–1994), left, walks with special advisor Henry A. Kissinger (b. 1923) in 1972. They are discussing ongoing peace talks in Paris. Nixon was first elected in 1968. He and Kissinger chose to prolong the war rather than withdraw from Vietnam and admit defeat.

Saigon and Hanoi

TWO VIETNAMS
Saigon and Hanoi were the main Vietnamese population centers. As a major seaport, Saigon was strongly influenced by cultures from other lands. Hanoi was influenced by the neighboring giant, China.

Fᴏʀ ᴄᴇɴᴛᴜʀɪᴇꜱ, Hᴀɴᴏɪ ᴡᴀꜱ ᴛʜᴇ ʟᴇᴀᴅɪɴɢ Vietnamese city. As the capital of French Indochina, Hanoi was a center of Vietnamese political, cultural, and economic life. The Communists made the city the DRV capital in 1954, but South Vietnam's capital, Saigon, soon passed Hanoi in wealth and population. A major commercial center, Saigon had long dominated southern Indochina's social and cultural life. As South Vietnam's military headquarters, Saigon boomed from American financial aid. Hanoi's streets were busy with bicycles and handcarts, but Saigon's roared with automobiles and motor scooters. Then, with war intensifying, many military vehicles appeared in both cities.

HANOI POLITICIANS
DRV prime minister Pham Van Dong (sitting at center) attends a 1946 Hanoi government meeting. Communists dominated the government, and many young people were active in Communist youth organizations. Yet, not all North Vietnamese were Communists.

Hanoi

During the French colonial period, Hanoi was famous for its restaurants and stylish upper class. After independence, the Hanoi region became a manufacturing center with first-rate schools and hospitals. Its several hundred thousand residents suffered many hardships in their struggle with France. Still, they fought on in the Vietnam War to unify their country.

WOMEN HOME GUARDS
An official registers female members of the Hanoi home guard, who are joining the army in 1964. Women were a large part of the home guard, which helped protect the city in time of conflict. This often included operating antiaircraft weaponry.

Communist flag

Pushcart

HANOI IN PEACEFUL TIMES
Few North Vietnamese owned motorized vehicles when they prepared for independence in 1954. Bicycles and pushcarts crowded this Hanoi street, with trolley rails in the center and Communist flags hanging from windows. Hanoi would soon be on its way to becoming a center for government, industry, and higher education.

Saigon

Under French rule, Saigon became a modern city with a powerful Vietnamese Roman Catholic elite—most Vietnamese were Buddhists. At the founding of the RVN in 1955, President Ngo Dinh Diem made Saigon the capital. The city grew rapidly as 900,000 northern Vietnamese fled Communist North Vietnam. U.S. money flowed into the RVN government and military, enriching the city's ruling class. Saigon was notorious for government corruption, gambling dens, prostitution, and the opium trade. By 1965, the city's population was 1.5 million and growing.

SAIGON'S OLD TOWN
The charm of 19th-century French colonial culture and architecture is seen in this 1955 Saigon street scene. A century of French influence made the city famous for its beauty. Saigon's culture, architecture, and nightlife earned her the name "Paris of the East."

HEROES RETURNING
Battle-weary ARVN soldiers marching in a Saigon parade are cheered up by pretty girls giving them garlands of flowers. The troops have just returned from operating against Viet Cong insurgents, in 1961.

U.S. soldier image

Scrip

SCRIP AND STOLEN GOODS
U.S. forces were given "scrip" (special money), to be spent only on military bases. However, scrip found its way into Saigon, where it was traded like dollars. There, goods stolen from U.S. bases were sold openly from street stalls.

American goods, smuggled or stolen for the black market

BUSTLING BOULEVARD
The avenues of central Saigon were clogged with motor scooters and automobiles in the mid-1960s. Still, the old-fashioned three-wheeled "peditaxi" in the foreground was a prime means of getting back and forth in the city. Handcarts powered by cyclists also were essential transport vehicles in overcrowded Saigon.

Rolling Thunder

THE TONKIN GULF INCIDENT and Viet Cong clashes with U.S. troops convinced LBJ's national security advisors that North Vietnam must be punished. Key advisor McGeorge Bundy believed that bombing the North would prove that the United States was determined to defend South Vietnam. The Operation Rolling Thunder bombing campaign began in March 1965. It targeted bridges, highways, railroads, airfields, factories, power plants, and fuel depots. Johnson called a temporary halt to the bombing seven times. He hoped halts would give the Communists a chance to ask for peace terms. They did not. Despite the damage, the Hanoi government continued its war effort and kept the supply chain to the VC flowing. Johnson ordered an end to the campaign on October 31, 1968.

McGEORGE BUNDY (1919–1996)
Bundy was a security advisor to Presidents Kennedy and Johnson. He urged the bombing campaign and helped plan it.

AIR FORCE THUNDERCHIEFS
Air Force F-105 Thunderchief fighter-bombers are refueled in the air while on their way to bomb North Vietnam, in 1966. The refueling aircraft, at right, is a KC-135 Stratotanker. Many U.S. fighter-bombers flew from bases thousands of miles away and had to refuel during their missions.

Stratotanker's drogue (refueling device) connects with fighter-bomber to pump in fuel

389th Tactical Fighter Squadron patch

STRATEGIC TARGETS
More than 643,000 tons of bombs were dropped on North Vietnam during Rolling Thunder, causing great destruction. U.S. aircraft avoided hitting major population areas around Hanoi and Haiphong, shown circled. LBJ wanted to minimize civilian casualties.

- Chinese buffer zone (prohibited to U.S. aircraft)
- ◯ Target restrictions around Hanoi and Haiphong
- — U.S. air attacks

SUCCESSFUL MISSION
Air Force commander George Jacobsen Jr. signals with the "okay" sign that he has completed a mission against NVA ammunition depots in 1965. Jacobsen had just landed safely on the carrier USS *Ranger*, operating off the Vietnamese coast. U.S. planes were limited to destroying military and economic targets during Rolling Thunder.

A-1 Skyraider warplane

Ammunition belt

Pilot helmet

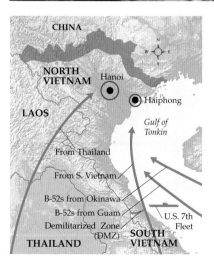

CHINA

NORTH VIETNAM
Hanoi

Haiphong

LAOS

Gulf of Tonkin

From Thailand

From S. Vietnam

B-52s from Okinawa

B-52s from Guam

Demilitarized Zone (DMZ)

U.S. 7th Fleet

THAILAND

SOUTH VIETNAM

BOMBS FALL

F-105 Thunderchiefs following a B-66 Destroyer over North Vietnam release their bombs. These small fighter-bombers attacked targets with great accuracy, while high-flying heavy bombers dropped payloads over a wider area. Fighter-bombers flew low to avoid NVA radar. Radar is an electronic system that sends out radio waves to detect objects at a distance. Planes flying lower than the radio waves are not detected.

AFTER A STRIKE

A North Vietnamese railroad bridge has partially collapsed after a U.S. air strike. Cutting railroads made it difficult for the Communists to transport equipment and troops. Whenever LBJ called a halt to bombing, the North Vietnamese hurried to rebuild their damaged factories and transportation links.

WILD WEASEL LANDING

This F-100 fighter's landing is slowed by a tail parachute. The aircraft is fitted with radar-jamming equipment that interferes with antiaircraft electronic devices. Nicknamed "Wild Weasels," these fighters specialized in finding and attacking surface-to-air missile (SAM) sites. They flew daringly low, through enemy fire, as they led other warplanes into action against North Vietnamese antiaircraft positions.

Parachute slows plane

Bridge collapsed from precision bombing

Wild Weasel patch

North Vietnam's air defense

With aid from the U.S.S.R. and China, Hanoi built a formidable antiaircraft defense. The small North Vietnamese Air Force also became increasingly effective during Rolling Thunder. Most of North Vietnam's warplanes and antiaircraft weapons were provided by its allies—as was training in their use and maintenance. During Rolling Thunder, more bombs were dropped on North Vietnam than the United States used in the Pacific Theater in World War II.

HOME GUARD

Young women in the Hanoi home guard search the skies for U.S. warplanes. Thousands of civilians were equipped with weapons and instructed to fire into the air. This created a storm of bullets to drive off or shoot down an attacker.

HANOI POSTCARD

The Hanoi government used postcards as propaganda tools. This card shows a peasant watching a stricken U.S. aircraft flaming to the ground. The pilot has parachuted clear, but will be captured.

Greeting from **VIETNAM**

THE VOICE OF VIETNAM
56-58 QUAN SU STREET — HANOI

Explosive warhead

AIMING A SAM

A surface-to-air guided missile crew on the outskirts of Hanoi prepares for a U.S. air attack. Thousands of trained Chinese SAM operators volunteered to serve in North Vietnam. SAMs were more than 30 feet (9 m) long, with 250 pounds (114 kg) of explosives. The U.S. campaign lost 922 aircraft, most of them shot down by SAMs and antiaircraft guns.

Machine gun

Concrete rim

AIR-RAID ALARM

A Hanoi resident takes cover in an air-raid shelter dug into the edge of a city street. Wailing sirens alerted people to immediately find shelter whenever U.S. planes were nearby. A piece of sheet metal is at hand, to be drawn over the hole for a cover if bombs fall.

Sheet metal cover

The Ho Chi Minh Trail

THIS NETWORK OF WILDERNESS ROUTES—named after Vietnam's nationalist hero—carried Communist equipment, supplies, and troops to fight in South Vietnam. The trail started near Hanoi, but was chiefly outside both Vietnams. The main trail wound into Laos, while another branch came through Cambodia. Many branches led into the South. Long sections passed through jungles that sheltered the trail from Allied bombing attacks. Antiaircraft batteries were placed along the way, and there were underground barracks, hospitals, workshops, and storage areas for munitions and fuel. Supplies moved by foot, bicycle, and even elephant. The network grew to 12,500 miles (20,000 km) of trails and roads. Much of it was paved for truck traffic. Late in the war, 3,000 miles (5,000 km) of pipeline carried fuel over mountains and under rivers. By 1970 more than 20,000 tons of supplies moved on the trail every month.

MUSCLE AND STEEL
NVA engineers fight rushing waters to lay steel girders for a new bridge in 1966. Footpaths and river fords were gradually replaced with roads and bridges for trucks. Much of the trail was designed and built by the NVA's Logistics Group 559. This unit gained international recognition for its work. More than 100,000 Vietnamese worked to build and maintain the trail.

NORTH VIETNAM

N
W · E
S

Demilitarized Zone (DMZ)

LAOS

● Hué
● Da Nang

THAILAND

Central Highlands

CAMBODIA

Mekong River
Phnom Penh ●

SOUTH VIETNAM

● Saigon
Mekong Delta

● Sihanoukville

South China Sea

 Ho Chi Minh Trail
Sihanouk Trail

STAIRWAY TO WAR
NVA troops carefully walk down steep wooden steps set against a mountain cliff. This unit is journeying near the DMZ in 1966. It will need two months to complete its march to a final position in South Vietnam. The Ho Chi Minh Trail was also referred to as the "Truong Son Road," because it entered the Truong Son Mountains of central Vietnam.

VAST ROUTE
Parts of the Ho Chi Minh Trail passed through Laos and Cambodia. Both stayed neutral during the war. Cambodia's Prince Norodom Sihanouk dared not block the trail, fearing to anger the Communists. Because he left the southern part of the trail alone, it was nicknamed "Sihanouk Trail."

BICYCLE WARFARE

Transport laborers on the Ho Chi Minh Trail use heavily loaded bicycles to haul ammunition for NVA troops in 1967. The bikes are fitted with specially designed handles for easier steering while being pushed along. The Communists could not have waged war without the trail to move supplies.

Specially adapted handles

SULFA DRUGS

Protecting the health of thousands of transport laborers, soldiers, and engineering corps workers was an essential task for the NVA. This Russian-made container for sulfa drugs was used by the North Vietnamese. Sulfa was for treating infection from parasites or bacteria, and for malaria.

VIET CONG SANDALS

While U.S. and ARVN soldiers had heavy boots and modern gear, Communist guerrillas used what they could salvage or make themselves. These sandals were cut from old rubber tires and tied with leather straps.

IN RAINY MOUNTAINS

Communist troops trekking on the trail toward South Vietnam cross misty mountains near the Laos-North Vietnam border. As many as 20,000 NVA troops moved southward on the Ho Chi Minh Trail every month. Thousands of soldiers and laborers died on the way, from air raids, disease, snakes—and even tigers.

CHINESE TELEPHONE

Communications on the trail depended on field telephones, such as this Chinese instrument captured from the VC by U.S. troops. Phones were installed at strongpoints or bunkers along the trail and linked by telephone cable.

1.5-volt dry-cell battery for power

Trees destroyed by U.S. bombing and defoliation campaigns

ROAD FOR TRUCKS

Supply trucks pass through a crossroads in a defoliated part of the trail in the 1970s. By this time, trucks were the heart of the transport system, carrying troops as well as supplies. NVA engineering battalions worked mainly by hand at first. They later received earthmoving and roadbuilding equipment from the Soviets and Chinese.

Napalm and Agent Orange

EARLY IN THE VIETNAM WAR, U.S. leaders called for eliminating the Viet Cong's support network in the countryside. This meant destroying food supplies and shelter, and driving out peasants who aided the VC. The military began to ruin vast areas of jungle and croplands by "defoliation"—killing all the leaves with chemical poisons. This exposed tree-covered guerrilla bases and supply routes to Allied aircraft. The weapons included "Agent Orange," a chemical defoliant sprayed over South Vietnam during a long-running air campaign. Also used were bombs containing napalm—an "incendiary" that burned all it touched. Defoliants and napalm turned once-beautiful and rich Vietnamese landscapes into wastelands.

WALTER W. ROSTOW
Top U.S. advisor Walter Rostow (1916–2003) urged Kennedy and Johnson to destroy areas of VC support, leading to the use of deadly defoliants and napalm.

MAKING NAPALM
A U.S. soldier mixes chemical thickeners into a drum of gasoline to make napalm, a jelly, in 1969. Upon exploding, flaming globules of napalm stick to everything they touch, causing great suffering. Flaming napalm also removes oxygen from the air, bringing injury and death to victims, who are unable to breathe.

DESTRUCTIVE PAYLOAD
Napalm bombs are mounted under the wing of an Air Force F-4 fighter-bomber at Da Nang airfield. Napalm was first used in World War II and set entire cities ablaze.

Napalm explosion

NAPALM EXPLOSIONS
Liquid fire blossoms into fireballs as a napalm strike from the air blasts a remote VC hamlet into ashes in 1965. The clinging flames of a napalm attack burn for hours afterward on trees and buildings. Napalm was a U.S. weapon of destruction widely used throughout the Vietnam War.

Ranch Hand's chemical assault

Operation Ranch Hand was the Air Force name for a campaign of spraying defoliants between 1962 and 1971. The defoliation squadron had just six aircraft at first, but grew to 25 by 1969. This was the peak of the campaign, which struck at VC bases in Cambodia as well as in South Vietnam. Streams of chemicals were sprayed on jungles and crop fields by slow-moving, low-flying, fixed-wing aircraft and helicopters. Most jungles could recover from two sprayings, but a third killed them. Mangrove swamps, however, died after only one spraying. More than 19 million gallons (72 million l) of herbicides were sprayed during the campaign—60 percent of it Agent Orange.

The C-123 aircraft was most commonly used in Ranch Hand

Trail of defoliant spray

RANCH HAND PATCH
The 12th Air Command Squadron carried out Ranch Hand missions. Members wore this patch marking their participation.

RANCH HAND
紫
VIETNAM

POISONOUS SPRAY
Low-flying aircraft spray herbicides over Communist-held country in Cambodia in 1966. Agent Orange can cause illness in humans. Both U.S. service members and Vietnamese civilians have lasting health problems from contact with such herbicides.

BEFORE AND AFTER
The effects of Ranch Hand defoliation are seen in this aerial photograph of land that has been sprayed and land left untouched. The field on the right side of the river is brown after being poisoned with Agent Orange. The left bank is still lush green.

CHOPPER-BORNE HERBICIDE
A Huey helicopter sprays a defoliation agent over jungle in the Mekong Delta, in 1969. Here, the U Minh Forest of mangrove swamps had a dense canopy—treetops—that hid people and buildings from aircraft. Herbicides destroyed this canopy and exposed VC positions.

Machine gunner

RIVER THROUGH RUIN
A Vietnamese paddles his boat between the bare banks of a former mangrove forest in the Mekong Delta, in 1970. Agent Orange destroyed swamps that once were bountiful for fishing and agriculture.

Sampan propelled by oars

Central Highlands struggle

CENTRAL HIGHLANDS
Central Highlands valleys could lead Communist forces down to the coast. Major battles were fought to control the Highlands, where U.S. bases blocked enemy movements.

THE RUGGED MOUNTAINS BETWEEN Cambodia and the sea—Vietnam's Central Highlands—were fought over during the entire war. Strongholds of Viet Cong and NVA were attacked by U.S. and Allied forces, but new ones soon arose. American bases in the region were under constant threat. Troops operating in the densely forested mountains could expect frequent ambushes. The Communists positioned soldiers and supplies in the Highlands, with the plan to break through to the seacoast one day. This would cut South Vietnam off from its northern provinces, which the Communists could then capture. Major battles in the Ia Drang Valley and at Dak To defeated the Communists, delaying their plans. The Americans found allies in the Montagnard people of the Central Highlands. U.S. Special Forces trained and armed the Montagnards, who proved especially brave.

NVA forces

NVA troops occupied large areas of the Central Highlands. They were trained in wilderness fighting and could move swiftly and silently. The Communists usually chose the time and place of battle in the mountains. The Americans and ARVN, however, won the major engagements during most of the war.

Communist star

Strap

NVA HELMET.
North Vietnamese soldiers wore cool and comfortable uniforms, with light but sturdy helmets that protected the wearer from sun and rain.

NGUYEN CHI THANH
General Thanh planned a major NVA offensive through the Central Highlands in 1965. His forces attempted to drive toward the sea, but they were defeated in battles in the Ia Drang Valley.

TUBULAR SCARF
The NVA soldier's daily ration of rice—his basic food—was carried in a hollow, tube-like scarf. Tied into a pouch, the scarf kept the rice secure.

Double spout

NVA OIL CAN
This two-compartment can held oil used to maintain weaponry.

Ammunition clip

AMMO POUCH
This ammunition belt with a harness is typical NVA "webbing," the term for military belts and pouches made of fabric. It holds three ammunition clips—magazines—and has pouches for bullets or tools.

Fastening loop

NVA CANTEEN
Communist fighters carried very little gear compared to heavily equipped U.S. and ARVN troops. The outgunned Communists had to travel fast and live off the land. A canteen for water was one of the most essential pieces of equipment.

Harness strap

Elite forces and allies

U.S. "Green Beret" Special Forces were active in the Central Highlands. Operating in small teams, they used guerrilla tactics against the NVA and made loyal allies of the native Montagnard peoples. The Montagnards (French for "mountain dwellers") were fiercely independent. They first opposed the South Vietnamese government, but the Special Forces arranged an alliance. Green Beret units equipped and trained the Montagnards and led them in battle. Other elite U.S. forces fighting in the Central Highlands included the troopers of the Air Cavalry (Air Cav) and Airborne. When the Special Forces camp at Dak To was threatened by the NVA in 1967, these troopers led the counterattack that defeated the Communists.

GUIDING A CHOPPER
A Green Beret waves in a supply helicopter landing near a smoke-grenade signal. The U.S. Special Forces' isolated mountain bases were resupplied by air, but the men often lived off the land. They ate what natives ate and faced danger every day.

Green beret

SETTING UP A HIGHLAND BASE
A Chinook transport helicopter supplies U.S. Airmobile troopers at a new mountaintop base in the Central Highlands in 1967. The Americans are on a search-and-destroy operation. The landing zone is codenamed LZ Quick. It will soon be discovered by the NVA, who will try to strike at the troopers with mortars and ambushes.

LAND NAVIGATION
This Green Beret wears a device known as a "position locator" to find his way through jungle. It has a "pedometer step sensor" that determines the length of his stride. Using a compass, the device tells the soldier precisely where he is in relation to where he started out.

AIRBORNE

Green Beret Airborne patch

Pedometer step sensor

M-60 machine gun

CAVALRY PATCH
This Air Cav regimental insignia bears the title of the 7th Cavalry Regiment's song: "Garry Owen."

Crossbow bolts

MONTAGNARD MEN
Montagnard soldiers armed with U.S. submachine guns prepare to go on patrol. They will search for signs of VC in their region and report back to the Americans. U.S. Special Forces teams began training Montagnards to fight Communists as early as 1963—during the advisory period of the Vietnam War.

Quiver

Wooden body

TAKING AIM
This 101st Airborne trooper is under fire during the battle of Dak To. Airborne and Air Cav troopers fought fiercely for three weeks. Victory was won on Thanksgiving Day.

MONTAGNARD CROSSBOW
This traditional handmade weapon of Vietnam's mountain people could be deadly in the counter-guerrilla warfare of the Central Highlands. It powerfully fired short arrows termed crossbow "bolts."

Weapons of war

The GROUND WAR IN VIETNAM was waged with many different weapons. Some were sophisticated and devastating, while others were primitive but deadly. Modern U.S. firearms were matched by weaponry provided to the Communists by the Soviets and Chinese. The Communists also used an ancient method: booby traps set on jungle trails. The support of villagers was essential to Viet Cong resistance in South Vietnam. Women helped make booby traps, and men repacked spent shell casings to make explosive mines. For all the power of U.S. Air Force bombing, the war was decided by ground action between foot soldiers. These bitter close-combat engagements required fierce courage on both sides.

CLAYMORE MINE
The U.S.-made Claymore antipersonnel mine fired 700 steel balls a hundred yards (90 m) in a 60-degree arc. The VC used captured Claymores against U.S. troops.

NVA GUN
South Vietnamese militiamen captured this 75-mm recoilless rifle from NVA troops.

NVA and VC forces

The Soviet Union and China provided North Vietnam with great quantities of arms and also sent instructors to teach their use. Wel armed NVA troops controlled portions of South Vietnam and operated in fairly large units. The VC, however, moved in small un in the shadow of U.S. and ARVN forces. VC often had to use weapo captured from their enemies. The captured Claymore antipersonne mine was one of the deadliest weapons used in VC ambushes.

BOMB-MAKING
VC soldiers salvage U.S. shell casings and unexploded artillery ammunition found on battlefields. Using hacksaws and grinding wheels, they reload the casings to make explosive devices. Grenades, above right, also were used in booby traps.

Grenades

Communist star

NVA knife

SOVIET-MADE AK-47
Rapid-firing AK-47 assault rifles were the most important firearms carried by Commun troops. Assault rifles gave individual soldiers tremendous firepower.

Ammunition magazine

SOVIET 7D GRENADE LAUNCHER
The shoulder-fired rocket-propelled grenade launcher ("RPG") is a powerful weapon. It can blast defenses apart, and some warheads can penetrate armor. The RPG allows infantrymen to destroy armored personnel carriers and attack tanks.

Rocket exhaust vent

Telescopic sight

Warhead holds explosive

Rocket-propelled grenade

Sharpened bamboo

BAMBOO STAKES
Villagers, above, sharpen bamboo into punji stakes that were used in booby traps. One method, right, was to set punjis in pits and cover them over with branches and leaves. The covering gave way when stepped on, and the individual fell into the pit.

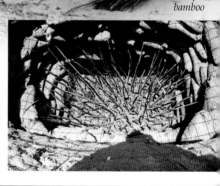

SKS SIMONOV CARBINE
Most SKS rifles were provided by China. The bayonet for this rifle could fold into a barrel support when the soldier fired lying down.

Trigger guard and magazine

Free World Forces

Soldiers of the Free World Forces used weapons similar to those of the Communists: assault rifles and grenade launchers. Although far better than weaponry the VC used, FWF weapons were matched by NVA arms. One advantage to Free World Forces was their artillery. For most of the war, the Communists had almost none in the field. Another advantage was the FWF's inexhaustible supplies. The Communists depended on the Ho Chi Minh Trail for resupply. Free World Forces had huge bases on the South Vietnamese coast. FWF troops in battle were resupplied by transport planes and helicopters.

Flash hider

M-1 bayonet

Launcher attached to end of barrel

Grenade and adaptor for M-1 carbine

Grenade

M1 CARBINE
ARVN troops often were equipped with older U.S. firearms, such as this M-1 carbine. Generally, the smaller, lighter carbine was easier for the more slightly built Vietnamese to use. The M-1 had a bayonet and fired rifle grenades as well as bullets.

30-round magazine

M-16 CLEANING KIT
Firearms must be perfectly maintained (cleaned and oiled) or they may not fire. This U.S. M-16 cleaning kit includes brushes to swab the inside of the rifle barrel.

Barrel of grenade launcher

Handle for cleaning rod

Sight for grenade launcher

Cleaning fluid

Cleaning brush attaches to rod

Hinge to fold rod compactly into a pouch

Cleaning brush

M-16 bayonet

Bayonet sheath

U.S. ASSAULT RIFLE
The M-16A1 offers more than the M-16 assault rifle's burst of automatic fire and 30-round magazine. The M-16A1 has a grenade launcher fixed under the muzzle. There is a separate sight and trigger for the grenade launcher. The combination offers greatly increased firepower in one weapon.

U.S. GRENADES
Infantry carried two or three grenades, which were thrown at the enemy and exploded. The ring for the pin was pulled, and after the soldier threw the grenade a fuse began to burn down. In a few seconds, the grenade exploded.

Pineapple grenade

Baseball grenade

Lemon grenade

Ring is pulled before throwing

Sight

Front sling fitting

GRENADE LAUNCHER
This U.S. M-79 grenade launcher, nicknamed "Blooper," has a range of 50–300 yards (46–274 m). This shoulder-fired weapon's grenade sends 300 metal fragments over an area 15 feet (5 m) in diameter.

Rear sling fitting

M-60 MACHINE GUN
A U.S. Special Forces soldier fires an M-60 7.62-mm machine gun at enemy positions. This belt-fed "general purpose" machine gun was one of the most important weapons available to American forces in Vietnam. It was used extensively to support small-unit operations and also was mounted on helicopters.

155-MM HOWITZER
ARVN artillerymen fire a 155-mm howitzer in the Central Highlands. Shells from a howitzer follow a high trajectory and drop onto enemy positions. Defenses that resist direct fire can be vulnerable to shells dropping down from above.

On patrol

THE U.S. MILITARY HAD ADVANCED WEAPONRY and powerful aircraft, but fighting in Vietnam required foot soldiers on patrol. Small groups of soldiers walked through dangerous areas known to have Communist activity. They patrolled rural villages where the people wanted protection from the Viet Cong or NVA. In these situations, patrols were often watched by hidden VC or NVA waiting for a chance to strike. Most patrols conducted "reconnaissance" (going out to learn the strength and location of enemy units). Reconnaissance patrols were usually in platoon or company strength of 20–100 men and went short distances. Patrols also might be part of a larger "search-and-destroy" mission, which tried to find Communists and kill or capture them. If a firefight began, a patrol's commander radioed the base for air or artillery support or reinforcement by chopper.

TAKING BEARINGS
An infantryman on patrol in unfamiliar territory uses a compass to determine his location. The Lensatic military compass has a front sight and a magnifying lens. The magnifier shows the compass dial's bearing when he sights on an object—perhaps a tree or a building. The compass folds into a carrying case.

Sighting wire, used with rear-sight slot and lens to sight on objects

Rear-sight slot

Lens is used to magnify dial

JUNGLE BOOTS
Waterproof boots were needed for patrolling in swampy jungles.

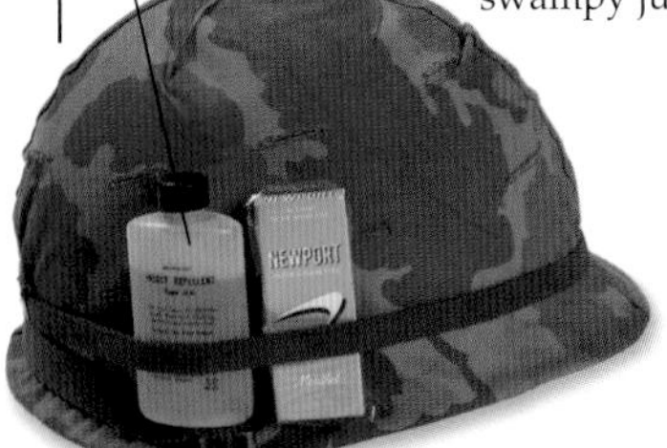

Insect repellent

Waterproof material

INFANTRY HELMET
The soldier's helmet strap was convenient for holding a pack of Army-issue cigarettes and bug repellent.

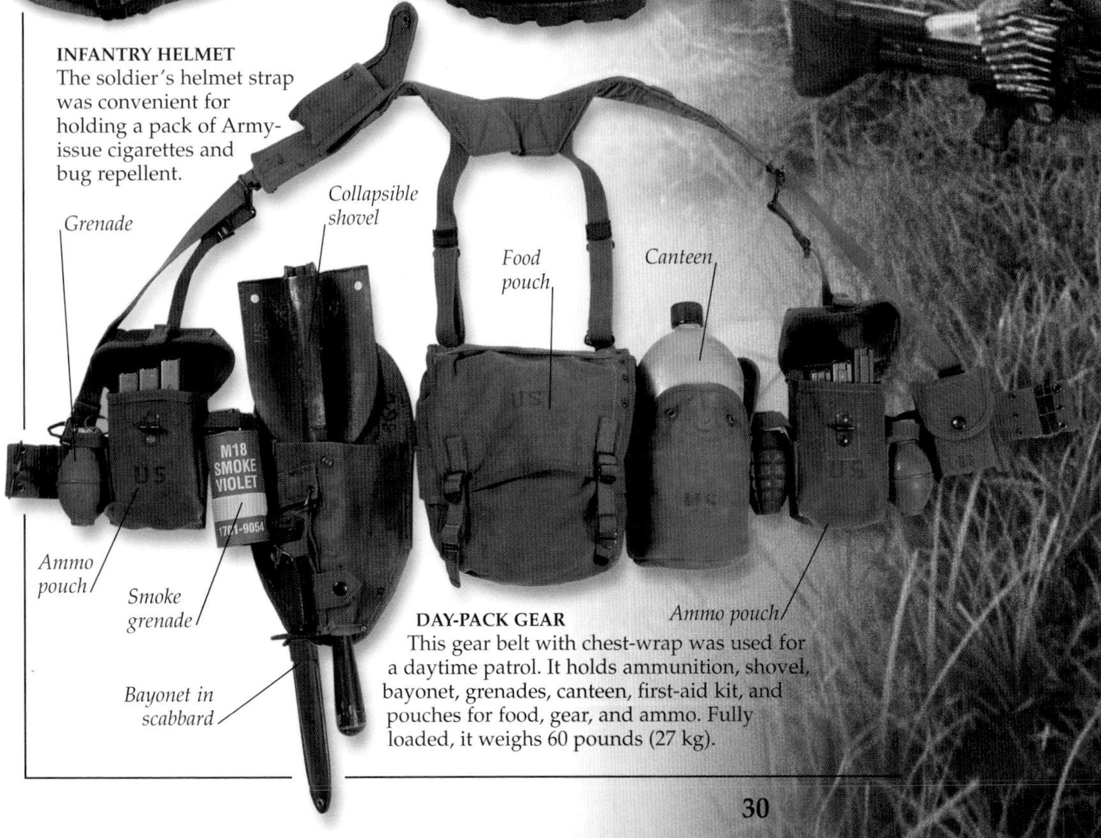

Grenade

Collapsible shovel

Food pouch

Canteen

Ammo pouch

Smoke grenade

M18 SMOKE VIOLET

Ammo pouch

Bayonet in scabbard

DAY-PACK GEAR
This gear belt with chest-wrap was used for a daytime patrol. It holds ammunition, shovel, bayonet, grenades, canteen, first-aid kit, and pouches for food, gear, and ammo. Fully loaded, it weighs 60 pounds (27 kg).

Short-range antenna

Radio controls

Long-range antenna

COLLECTING WATER
A 1st Infantry Division soldier on patrol refills his canteen at a flowing stream. Small 1.3-quart (1.25 l) canteens were used on short patrols, while five-quart (4.75 l) canteens were used on long-range patrols. Water was made safe to drink by adding halazone, a powder that killed bacteria.

CALLING THE BASE
A radioman, left, carries a backpack field radio while his commanding officer uses the handset to report to headquarters. Patrols usually set out from fire bases—fortified encampments with headquarters, artillery, and support troops. A patrol could radio the base for VC or NVA positions to be shelled or to request reinforcements or medevacs.

PRC 9 backpack field radio

Handset (phone)

Five-quart inflatable canteen

Vial of halazone water purifier

Instructions for inflating canteen

VC ambush

The Viet Cong were skilled at laying ambushes for approaching patrols. They hid in trees, in fields, and even underground. They often struck from all sides with a hail of gunfire and grenades. The leading man of the patrol—the soldier on point—was in particular danger from a surprise attack. If outnumbered, ambushers would soon melt into the countryside. If superior in force, they would try to wipe out the patrol before air support arrived.

IN THE OPEN
Troops of the 9th Infantry Division turn toward possible enemy movement as they walk across a rice paddy. Patrols were exposed to surprise attacks, especially as they entered forests, approached villages, or crossed open fields. This is a "day patrol," since the soldiers carry little gear or supplies. "Long-range reconnaissance patrols" went into the field for several days, often as part of search-and-destroy operations.

WATCHING AND WAITING
A VC fighter lies in a forest ditch, rifle at the ready. He is part of a force waiting silently to ambush a U.S. or ARVN patrol.

DEMONSTRATING TACTICS
Posing for the camera, VC guerrillas show how to hide under haystacks. In combat, they would withdraw completely under the hay if an enemy patrol approached. If the patrol were too strong, the guerrillas would let it pass, hoping not to be discovered. Otherwise, they would attack on command.

Medical care and evacuation

As soon as the Vietnam conflict began, the American military rapidly expanded its medical service. In 1965, the United States had only two military hospitals in Vietnam, with 100 beds each. By 1969, there were approximately 30 U.S. hospitals, with 5,000 beds, and two Navy hospital ships. These hospitals were staffed by 16,000 doctors, 15,000 nurses, and thousands of support personnel. On the battlefield, soldiers termed "medics" bandaged the wounded and called for helicopter airlifts. These emergency flights, known as "medevacs" (medical evacuations) quickly brought the injured to hospitals for immediate care. Communist field forces had primitive medical units. Their wounded were slowly carried to field hospitals hidden in swamps, caves, or tunnels.

MEDEVAC BUCKLE
"Dustoff" on this pilot's belt buckle is a nickname for ambulance helicopters, which landed and took off quickly.

Extra bandages

MEDIC'S KIT
The foot soldier's medic carried first-aid gear to treat wounds in the field. His kit included bandages, gauze, tape, antiseptics, cotton swabs, and medical status cards to identify the patient and document injury.

U.S. FIELD MEDICAL CARD

PLAIN ABSORBENT GAUZE

Medical status cards

SMALL FIELD BROWN FIRST-AID DRESSING

Wires to attach medical cards to patients

ADHESIVE TAPE

Wire splint for broken arm or leg

First-aid tape

Gauze bandages

Sterilized brown first-aid dressing

MEDEVAC CHOPPER ARRIVES
A medical evacuation helicopter comes in to pick up wounded troops in 1966. The pilot homes in on the purple cloud of a smoke grenade that signals where to land. A soldier extends his arms to guide the pilot onto solid ground. After loading the wounded and taking off, this chopper might come under gunfire. Many Americans were treated within 20 minutes of being injured.

M18 SMOKE VIOLET

1701-9054

Purple smoke grenade

EVACUATING A WOUNDED SOLDIER
An injured Marine is helped to safety as a medic holds a blood transfusion kit to replace lost blood. Improved medical technology resulted in fewer than one in five U.S. wounded dying from injuries. In World War II, one in three died from their wounds.

Rigid litter basket

BASKET FOR CASUALTIES
A U.S. Army helicopter lowers a rigid litter basket to be loaded with a seriously wounded soldier in October 1967. Often, medical helicopters could not land in dense jungles that did not have clearings. Litters were lowered by steel cables, and the wounded were hauled up and swiftly flown away from the battlefield.

SAVING A LIFE
A U.S. Army team of doctors and nurses performs an emergency operation in a surgical hospital in 1969. Male doctors were usually drafted into the military, but female staff were volunteers. Seriously injured patients would be flown to large military hospitals in Japan or Okinawa for further treatment.

FIRST STOP FOR WOUNDED
Medics carry an injured soldier on a stretcher from a medevac helicopter that has just landed at a field hospital. The chopper's red cross symbolizes a medical unit, which should not be fired upon. Medevac helicopters were shot at anyway, and some were lost.

President George Washington

DOG TAGS
Nicknamed "dog tags," these metal tags are stamped with personal data to identify a soldier if he is wounded or killed. All troops must wear dog tags on chains around their necks.

PURPLE HEART
This medal is given to all U.S. military injured in combat. More than 200,700 Purple Hearts were awarded during the Indochina conflict.

Blood pressure cuff

Mosquito netting

Communist medical units

With Americans or ARVN controlling the air, Communist field hospitals in South Vietnam were camouflaged to prevent bombing attacks. There were few safe areas for treatment of the wounded. Their sparse medical supplies usually came from China or the U.S.S.R. and were carried over long backcountry trails. Viet Cong and NVA fighters suffered greatly from tropical sickness and fever because they served long periods in dark, steamy jungles.

Wooden pole for carrying hammock with patient

Chinese penicillin bottle, 1½ inches (3.8 cm) tall

JOURNEY FOR AID
With no helicopters of their own, Communist soldiers lug a wounded comrade to an aid station. They carry a litter made from a hammock suspended on a bamboo pole and have to trek two hours through difficult terrain to the nearest medical facility.

Wood and canvas stretcher

OPERATING IN A SWAMP
Viet Cong nurses and doctors working in a secret field hospital prepare to operate in 1970. Their facility is hidden in a mangrove swamp, knee-deep in water. The stretcher-bearer awaits orders from the staff to bring the patient, a young guerrilla, to the operating table.

Heliborne warfare

MILITARY HELICOPTERS CAME INTO WIDE USE during the Vietnam War, termed the "Helicopter War." Until then, helicopters had been used only for scouting and for airlifting wounded. By the 1960s, U.S. helicopters were redesigned and improved in power and armaments. Nicknamed "choppers" because of their rotating blades, they rushed soldiers into action, fired at enemy positions, and transported equipment and supplies. Helicopters gave U.S. and ARVN forces a great advantage because the NVA had no helicopters of their own.

HARRY W. O. KINNARD (b. 1915)
General Kinnard led the 1st Cavalry Division, which was the first military unit to be transported by helicopter. Known as "airmobile" or "heliborne" troops, Kinnard's division went to Vietnam in 1965.

M-16 rifle

Landing

Supply pouch

AIR CAVALRY RIDE IN ON CHOPPERS
Troopers of the 1st Air Cavalry Division hit the ground running as they jump down from a "Huey" helicopter during a scouting mission. "Air Cav" troopers were the world's first trained heliborne soldiers. Their success in Vietnam led to the widespread use of military helicopters and the creation of more airmobile units.

ROCKET ON TARGET
A rocket flashes from a U.S. Navy helicopter, seen from above as it attacks an NVA position. This type of chopper was nicknamed "Huey," after its model name: UH-1. Chopper covering-fire from the air supported ground troops, who communicated by radio to call in helicopters during combat.

HUEY WEAPONRY
The Huey's armaments included seven-pod aerial-rocket launchers, at right, and also rapid-firing machine guns, such as the "minigun" at left.

Rockets

Helicopter wing

Machine gun ammunition belt

GUNNER DUTY
A machine gunner looks for Viet Cong while flying over South Vietnam. Helicopter gunners were favorite enemy targets. Their duty was considered one of the most dangerous of the war.

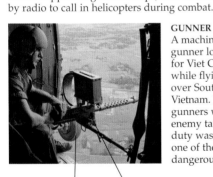

Helicopter landing wheel

Heavy machine gun

Pilot and co-pilot positions

Fuselage and tail

COBRA ATTACK HELICOPTER
This Marine Corps AH-1W Sea Cobra was one of the first models designed as an attack helicopter. The first AH-1s came into service in 1967. These "gunships" were specially built for escorting fast-moving transport helicopters. Although the heavily armed UH-1 Huey was the military's main workhorse helicopter, it was too slow to keep up with the transport choppers. AH-1 Cobras were swift and maneuverable, with great firepower. They were employed by the Marines and the Army during the war.

*Pilot and
co-pilot positions*

Cannon

AIR CAVALRY INSIGNIA
Helicopter pilots and mechanics
wore patches that distinguished
them from the division's troopers.
These units of the 7th Squadron,
1st Cavalry Regiment, nicknamed
themselves "Apache Aeroscouts"
and "King Birds."

Apache Aeroscouts

King Birds

Cargo helicopters

The Americans and ARVN operated thousands of helicopters
during the war, with four main models: "utility" for general
use; "observation" for scouting; "attack" gunships for battle,
and "cargo" for transporting materials. The cargo helicopter
was needed everywhere, ferrying supplies and
equipment around the country. New models
were constantly improved in carrying-capacity,
with more powerful engines.

CHINOOK AT WORK
The mighty CH-47 Chinook
helicopter was one of the best
cargo aircraft of the war. The
most frequently transported
freight of these heavy-lifting helicopters were field guns.
One such gun is shown suspended beneath the body
of a U.S. Army Chinook, in flight to a distant base.

Landing wheel

Cannon barrel

Cannon limber

Field cannon

FLYING CRANE
This CH-54A Skycrane transport helicopter was
termed a "Flying Crane" for its ability to lift heavy
equipment and weapons. Loads were carried
in the cutaway under the fuselage. The Skycrane
often moved guns and vehicles into isolated
bases, where soldiers built fortifications
and artillery positions to
prepare for battle.

Rotors

Tail-mounted rotor

*Cutaway design
for large cargo*

*Tall landing
gear for cutaway*

Warplanes in combat

T HE "ROLLING THUNDER" BOMBING campaign struck North Vietnamese roads, railroads, and bridges. This slowed the movement of Communist military supplies. Bombing population centers was not permitted, though, because LBJ did not want civilian casualties. This was why he did not use high-altitude heavy bombers that would cause widespread destruction. Most missions were carried out by F-105 fighter-bombers. These flew lower and were easier targets for antiaircraft fire. By the end of 1966, 455 U.S. warplanes had been shot down. The small North Vietnamese Air Force (NVAF) steadily improved. Its high-speed Soviet-made MiG-21 "interceptors" had downed 10 bombers and damaged many others. In January 1967, superior U.S. fighters won a dramatic victory over the MiG-21s. By the end of 1967, the bombing campaign had devastated North Vietnam, but 649 U.S. aircraft had been lost.

FIGHTER PILOT
The glow of the instrument panel lights the face of a U.S. F-4 fighter pilot. He is preparing to take off on a night mission from Da Nang air base.

F-4D Phantom cockpit

Flight helme

Star symboliz a kil

AMERICAN ACE
Captain Charles B. DeBellevue was the war's top U.S. fighter pilot, or "ace." He flew 220 combat missions and won his title by shooting down six MiGs

Tricking NVAF defenders

The NVAF's MiG-21s took on the less-maneuverable F-105 fighter-bombers but avoided the faster F-4 Phantoms. On January 2, 1967, Colonel Robin Olds led his 8th Tactical Fighter Wing in "Operation Bolo." Intending to draw MiG-21s into action, his F-4 fighters flew in the same formation, speed, and altitude as F-105 fighter-bombers. They also used F-105 radio call-signs. MiG-21s rose and were surprised to find themselves facing F-4 Phantoms. Seven MiG-21s were shot down, with no American losses.

U.S. Air Force symbol on aircraft

Fuselage

Colonel's eagle

Rear horizontal wing stabilizes plane

Air-to-air missile

Harness for parachute

Vest with pouches

Inflation hose controls air pressure in flight suit

OPERATION BOLO LEADER
Colonel Robin Olds commanded the 8th Tactical Fighter Wing. He shot down one of the seven MiG-21s destroyed over North Vietnam during Operation Bolo. Olds eventually shot down four enemy aircraft. He earned the Air Force Cross, right, awarded for extraordinary heroism.

Flight suit

Air Force Cross

Bald eagle symbolizes America States and air striking power.

MIG-KILLERS
F-4 Phantoms fly in close formation while on patrol over Southeast Asia in 1967. This formidable fighter escorted the older and less maneuverable F-105 fighter-bombers in bombing missions over North Vietnam. The F-4 was the best fighter of the day, flying at speeds of 1,600 mph (2,500 kmph). They were termed "MiG killers." A total of 42 F-4s were lost in the Vietnam War.

DOGFIGHT
Viewed through the 20mm cannon sight of a pursuing F-105, a MiG is hit on the wing. The older F-105 fighter-bombers were often at a disadvantage to NVAF MiGs in aircraft-to-aircraft engagements known as "dogfights." This F-105 next passed 20 feet (7 m) beneath the doomed MiG.

NVAF ACE
Pham Thanh Ngan was the fourth-leading NVAF ace, having shot down eight U.S. warplanes. He wears an Air Medal for each kill. NVAF pilots were trained by China and the U.S.S.R. and flew aircraft made by those countries. Ngan flew a Soviet MiG-21, the best NVAF fighter.

Ho Chi Minh

AIR MEDAL
NVAF pilots received this medal for shooting down Allied aircraft.

Air Medal

PREPARING FOR TAKEOFF
In the cockpit of his MiG-21, third-best NVAF ace Mai Van Cuong readies for a mission. Cuong recorded eight kills, while the top NVAF ace, Nguyen Van Coc, had nine. MiG-21s were flown by 12 of the 16 NVAF aces. A pilot is declared an ace after he has five kills. The NVAF's 16 aces accounted for 106 of the 169 U.S. warplanes shot down in air-to-air combat.

MiG cockpit

Cockpit cover

AIR BASE
A ground crew services a fighter at a North Vietnamese airfield on the outskirts of Hanoi. Since U.S. bombers stayed away from Hanoi's population areas, NVAF aircraft were based near the city to avoid being bombed.

20-mm cannon sight

Second cockpit for weapons system officer

Pilot's cockpit

Engine exhaust

M-61A1 20-mm cannon

Nose

Serial number

SOVIET MIG-21
This MiG-21 fighter is on exhibit at a museum in Hanoi. The MiG-21 was designed as a fast interceptor to pursue, catch, and drive off attacking enemy aircraft. This highly maneuverable fighter flew at 1,385 mph (2,200 kmph) and was armed with air-to-air missiles. It was a "short-range" fighter, meant for defensive missions close to its home base. Between 1965 and 1973, U.S. warplanes downed 68 MiG-21s. Few NVAF fighter pilots survived the war.

NVAF symbol on aircraft

Landing gear

The Television War

THE VIETNAM WAR WAS CALLED the first "Television War," because television brought the horrors of war into American homes as never before. News reporting influenced how Americans understood the war. At first, most U.S. journalists working in Vietnam supported the war. They reported on the military situation but did not explain Vietnam's long struggle against foreign rule. As the conflict became worse, the U.S. government pretended it was going well. Then some influential journalists, such as Walter Cronkite, turned against the war and called for peace negotiations. Meanwhile, the North Vietnamese press tried to influence world opinion to oppose the war.

AT THE TYPEWRITER
Reporter Neil Sheehan writes about the Vietnam conflict in 1963. Sheehan first reported for the news service United Press International (UPI) and then for *The New York Times*. He later exposed government lies about the war.

Bronze Star

FIGHTING REPORTER
UPI's Joseph Galloway often fought alongside the troops he covered. Galloway won a Bronze Star medal for carrying a wounded man to safety.

News film camera

Microphone

Helmet with AP logo

AIMING WITH A CAMERA
Vietnamese photographer Huynh Thanh My lies in muddy water under enemy fire while on assignment for the news service Associated Press (AP). My covered ARVN troops fighting in the Mekong Delta in 1965. He was killed later that year on a similarly risky assignment.

Sound monitor

INTERVIEWING SOLDIERS
Reporters and cameramen from CBS television news interview U.S. soldiers about a recent battle in 1967. American military commanders gave journalists in Vietnam considerable freedom to travel around and meet with the troops.

YOUNG PHOTOJOURNALIST
Twelve-year-old Lo Manh Hung checks his camera while taking pictures in Saigon, in 1968. At the age of 10, this Vietnamese youth began working with his father—a veteran photojournalist. Hung wears a military helmet—proof of the danger he often faced. His helmet is labeled with "Press" in both English and Vietnamese.

HELPING THE INJURED
In 1975 UPI photographer Willy Vicoy carries a wounded girl to safety after heavy rocketing near Cambodia's capital, Phnom Penh. A U.S. Navy vessel has just transported the child and her family away from the bombing. Correspondents and photographers often put off covering events to take part in them, usually to help the injured or elderly.

Stars and Stripes Correspondent patch

NEWS ABOUT HIS WAR
A 9th Division soldier reads the Army's daily newspaper, *Stars and Stripes,* which tells of military action and antiwar protests. This paper was respected for reporting what soldiers wanted to know about the war and politics.

PRESS PASS
MACV issued press cards to "war correspondents," as journalists were termed. Frances FitzGerald's reporting won her fame.

Department of Defense seal

NVA PRESS CONFERENCE
Viet Cong general Tran Van Tra holds a press conference near the battlefront. Like the Americans and South Vietnamese, Communist officials strictly limited information about the war. Newspapers were the main North Vietnamese source of news. The nation's first television network, Vietnam Television, went into service in 1970.

PENTAGON CONFERENCE
U.S. secretary of defense Robert McNamara faces microphones at the Pentagon in 1967 as he answers journalists' questions about the war. The government's daily press conferences often gave reporters overly optimistic or misleading reports. This caused many journalists to mistrust the information.

Map of Vietnam

WALTER CRONKITE AND VIETNAM
Highly respected CBS television anchorman Walter Cronkite reports on the Vietnam War in 1968. Cronkite dismayed many Americans by comparing the destruction and loss in the Vietnam conflict to World War II, which he had covered. Cronkite criticized U.S. military policy, and LBJ grumbled, "If I've lost Cronkite, I've lost middle America."

EXPOSING THE TRUTH
In 1971, former Pentagon staffer Daniel Ellsberg gave *The New York Times* secret documents detailing government lies about the war. Neil Sheehan and other journalists reported on the documents in a series of articles titled "The Pentagon Papers." Most Americans were now convinced the war should be stopped.

MEKONG DELTA
The 2,800-mile (4,500 km) Mekong River deposits fine soil as it empties into the South China Sea, building up a delta (sandy lowland). Near the Mekong Delta is Saigon, South Vietnam's largest city. The areas shaded in blue on the map show U.S. and ARVN riverine operations against the VC.

The Mekong Delta

THE MEKONG DELTA OF SOUTHERN VIETNAM is Indochina's "rice bowl." Much of the delta is covered with waterlogged paddies—fields of rice, the most important food in Asia. The delta is at the mouth of the Mekong River and covers 26,000 square miles (67,340 sq. km). Crisscrossed by muddy channels and streams, the delta was a guerrilla stronghold throughout the Indochina wars. In the Vietnam War, U.S. and ARVN forces established military bases to control the delta's scattered villages—often built on poles above the water. Gunboats trying to find and destroy Viet Cong bases passed along the waterways, while infantry patrolled on foot. Aircraft scouted for the guerrillas, then struck at their positions or supply routes. The VC retreated from superior forces, but returned to fight again. They held on throughout the war, aided by a population that for the most part supported their cause.

STRIKE MISSION
Flames and smoke rise from a rocket attack by an American UH-18 Iroquois helicopter in the Mekong Delta. Twisting waterways and patchwork rice paddies are surrounded by dense woods that shelter VC guerrillas.

Flames from rocket strike

UNDER A GUN
An ARVN armored personnel carrier's heavy machine gun aims at the Mekong Delta horizon as a farmer plows his rice paddy. The government often destroyed rice crops in order to keep VC guerrillas from sharing farmers' food. Losing their crops angered farmers, and many turned against the government to side with the VC.

Swamp buffalo serve as draft animals for rice cultivation

VC FIGHTER
Guerrilla sentry Soc Trang stands at her post in the Mekong Delta in 1973. Trang was only 24 years old but already had been widowed twice. Both husbands had been VC soldiers who died in action. The VC and North Vietnamese forces counted many women among their fighters bearing arms in the field. Trang has a captured U.S. M-16 rifle.

MEKONG HAMLET
This view from a low-flying aircraft in 1968 shows a remote hamlet surrounded by the waters of the Mekong River. The river flows slowly here and is just a few feet deep beside the houses. Boats are the main transportation, but houses are linked by built-up paths that have been used for centuries.

Path between houses

Thatched roof

POLING HOMEWARD
Mekong Delta family members use long poles to push a boat through the shallow waters that surround their hamlet. A neighbor building a new house works on the roof's ridge pole. The typical hamlet home is framed with poles that are covered with a thatched roof—usually a blanket of dried leaves or straw held down by rope and more poles. These houses stand on earthen bases above the water level.

Captured U.S. M-16 rifle

Poles support racks for drying fishing nets

SOLDIER'S PATCH
This uniform patch is from the U.S. 9th Infantry Division, which served in the Mekong. This was a difficult service, with frequent VC ambushes and a hot, steamy climate.

MONITOR IN THE MEKONG
A heavily armed and armored Monitor gunboat churns slowly past a large village in the Mekong Delta during an operation against the VC. The U.S. Navy gunboat is heading for a nearby base, where other military craft are gathered to support the operation. The crewmen and soldiers of a U.S. vessel docked just up ahead watch the gunboat approach.

41

War on inland waters

Early in 1965, the U.S. Navy began patrolling South Vietnam's 3,000 miles (4,800 km) of inland waterways. Many Vietnamese rivers, canals, and streams were narrow and jungle-covered, and Viet Cong ambushes made them dangerous to enter. In the swampy Mekong and Saigon river deltas, Communist forces dominated thousands of remote villages and farms. To penetrate these strongholds, MACV headquarters established a joint Army-Navy task force. In 1967, the Mobile Riverine Force—"riverine" means operating along waterways—went into action. It combined Army troops with the crews of fast Navy patrol boats, armored gunboats and troop carriers, and napalm-firing boats. Larger vessels served as floating barracks that followed the action inland. Riverine units were nicknamed the "Brown Water Navy" since they operated in muddy waterways. The Brown Water Navy struck deep into enemy territory, opening much of the delta region to Saigon government control.

ELMO R. ZUMWALT JR. (1920–2000)
Called the "Father of the Brown Water Navy," which he helped establish, Admiral Zumwalt commanded U.S. naval forces in Vietnam from 1968 to 1970.

NAVAL PATCHES OF VIETNAM
Each naval unit had a distinctive uniform patch. Sailors of the USS *White River*, a World War II-era warship, wore a design with an eagle perched on an early naval cannon. Task Force 116, also called the River Patrol Force, wore a round patch with a shield, lightning bolts, and swords. River Assault Division 91 wore a patch showing a fighting "River Rat" riding a patrol boat.

USS *White River* naval patch

River Assault Division 91 patch

Patch of the River Patrol Force, Task Force 116

GUNBOAT IN THE MEKONG
A "Monitor" patrols the Mekong Delta near Saigon in 1967. These armored vessels were named after Union gunboats of the U.S. Civil War.

Frame for canvas roof

50-mm cannon

Rotating armored gun turret

Reinforced steel hull

Loading ramp falls forward onto river bank when landing troops

PATROLLING THE MEKONG
A U.S. Navy task force churns through the waters of the Viet Cong-held Mekong Delta in late 1967. These heavily armored river assault boats were part of the joint Army-Navy Mobile Riverine Force. They are moving down a canal in one of several missions code-named Operation Coronado, which inflicted heavy losses on the enemy.

Thick steel armor protects troops

Pole used to propel craft and for steering

ARVN RIDE A SAMPAN
South Vietnamese troops, in the southern province of Ca Mau, South Vietnam, return to camp in a native craft loaded with firewood. South Vietnam had a modern navy, but its riverine forces often used the traditional sampan, powered by oars or by poling in shallow waters.

A ZIPPO BLASTS ENEMY POSITIONS

The Navy's deadly flame boats were nicknamed "Zippos," after a popular brand of cigarette lighter. Guns on the Zippo's turrets shot streams of flaming napalm up to 200 yards (180 m), destroying everything within range. Napalm is a jelly that sticks to its target and keeps on burning. In ambushes, the Viet Cong often attacked the dangerous Zippos first to knock them out of action.

BURNING OUT VC

Primitive but effective, the flaming arrow being fired from this American officer's bow will set the straw roofs of a Viet Cong riverbank base on fire. Such strikes avoided the need to land troops.

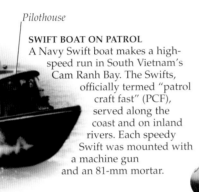

Radar mast

Deckhouse

Pilothouse

SWIFT BOAT ON PATROL

A Navy Swift boat makes a high-speed run in South Vietnam's Cam Ranh Bay. The Swifts, officially termed "patrol craft fast" (PCF), served along the coast and on inland rivers. Each speedy Swift was mounted with a machine gun and an 81-mm mortar.

Shark-tooth bow design

SHARK-MOUTHED HOVERCRAFT

Fiercely decorated, fast-moving patrol air cushion vehicles (PACVs) crossed swamps and waterlogged rice paddies where no other vehicle could go. These hovercraft transported troops for surprise assault missions and could move quickly to block enemy escape routes. This PACV's cushion of forced air lifts it across dry land.

Villages in wartime

VIETNAMESE PEASANTS IN THE COUNTRYSIDE lived much like their ancestors. The seasonal cycles of plowing, planting, harvesting, and fishing shaped daily life—but war too often caused suffering. VC fighters depended on support from the villagers and threatened those who did not cooperate with them. U.S. and ARVN troops, in turn, ordered villagers not to aid the VC. The Saigon government built defenses and walls around some communities to keep VC out. Peasants tried to carry on farming, but soldiers of both sides often punished them for helping the opposition. In 1968, U.S. troops massacred hundreds of civilians in the village of My Lai. When the news reached America, many more people turned against the war.

STRATEGIC HAMLETS
In the early 1960s, South Vietnam built fortified towns guarded by civilian militia, shown at left. These "strategic hamlets" were surrounded by fences and ditches, visible in this aerial view. Peasants were forced to move in to keep them from the VC. Yet most wanted to go home, and the program ended after a few years.

Sharpened bamboo

COMING CLOSE
A U.S. Army scout helicopter drops down low to investigate villagers tending buffalo in a meadow. ARVN troops are approaching in the background. Peasants never knew whether soldiers in passing helicopters would think they were VC and suddenly fire on them. Living in a combat zone exposed farmers to danger every day.

AFTER ACTION
ARVN soldiers talk with peasants in a rural village soon after an engagement with VC guerrillas. The soldiers had just fought off a VC ambush, and an ARVN lieutenant was killed. The officer's body lies in the bottom of the boat being poled into the village. If the soldiers think any of these villagers helped the VC, their huts will likely be burned.

ON TRIAL
A jungle village's "people's court" led by the VC tries a young man accused of aiding the ARVN. Villagers hear the charges before voting on a verdict. The youth was found guilty and sentenced to two years in prison. A companion put on trial along with him was sentenced to death.

PACIFICATION PROGRAM
A Marine chaplain demonstrates a toy trumpet to Vietnamese children. Bringing toys, food, and humanitarian aid—such as medical care—was part of a relief program organized by the United States known as the Pacification Program. The military wanted to "win the hearts and minds" of the people by trying to earn their trust.

Dwellings

Shoulder basket

SEARCHING FOR COMMUNISTS
Air Cavalry troopers cautiously search a house for signs of NVA or VC soldiers. The troopers are on patrol in the rugged Central Highlands, where NVA troops operated in large numbers. The Air Cav has the mission to clear out the Communists, whose agents could be hiding among civilians.

CHORES IN A WAR ZONE
Peasant women carrying shoulder baskets meet U.S. Marines assembling on a road. The women keep to the middle as the troops part to let them through.

Massacre at My Lai

Soldiers of the U.S. Army Americal Division entered the hamlet of My Lai on March 16, 1968, with orders to burn it. The troops believed the villagers were VC sympathizers. Under the command of Lt. William L. Calley Jr., they herded more than 300 men, women, and children together and shot them down. Other villagers were saved when a U.S. helicopter crew threatened to fire on Calley's men. The military tried to cover up the massacre but the story leaked out. Several soldiers were tried for murder, but only Calley was convicted. He was immediately released on parole.

FIRE AND DEATH
After killing hundreds of civilians, Americal Division soldiers burn the hamlet of My Lai. There were no reports of the troops having come under attack. A year later, a former soldier wrote a letter to President Nixon, the Pentagon, and members of Congress about the atrocity, which became public. Many Americans were outraged, and the antiwar movement gained strength.

CALLEY TO COURT
William Calley, center, and his military and civilian attorneys arrive for a pretrial hearing in Fort Benning, Georgia, in January 1970. A large number of Americans believed Calley should not have been punished because both sides had killed so many civilians. Calley was sentenced to life imprisonment, but President Nixon arranged to have the sentence reduced to 20 years. Later, Nixon granted Calley parole after the officer had spent only three days in a military jail.

Tunnels

THE VIETNAMESE BEGAN digging tunnels during the First Indochina War. These were used as bomb shelters and places for anti-French guerrillas to hide weapons. Tunneling continued during the Vietnam War in Communist-controlled areas of South Vietnam. Guerrilla fighters and their supporters lived for long periods underground in complex tunnel systems. The largest networks included sleeping rooms, kitchens, ammunition depots, hospitals, and meeting halls. When U.S. or Allied troops passed by, fighters hid in the tunnels or else came out for surprise attacks. Allied forces sent courageous volunteers, armed only with pistols and knives, into the tunnels to find out if they were being used.

VIET CONG DIG TUNNELS
Vietnamese laborers use primitive tools to hand-dig an entrance to a tunnel system. They lift out dirt-filled reed baskets, empty them, then send them back down for more. When completed, this part of the tunnel will be covered over, hidden from the surface.

Wooden plug — *Shrapnel pieces*

VC antipersonnel mine

Trigger mechanism

BOOBY TRAPS
The VC set traps to injure enemy troops coming into a tunnel. Traps included mines detonated by a trip wire, and even poisonous snakes, such as vipers or cobras. Snakes kept in bamboo stalks would be released if the stalks were accidentally knocked out of place by anyone crawling through.

Chinese cobra

TUNNELS AT CU CHI
The largest tunnel complex was at Cu Chi, 45 miles (75 km) north of Saigon. Here were more than 155 miles (250 km) of tunnels. This illustration, on display at the Cu Chi Museum's visitor center, shows how many parts a tunnel system could have. They were several levels deep, with electricity, underwater entrances, air shafts, sentry posts, and a headquarters.

Hidden entrance — *Underwater entry* — *Guard post* — *Air shafts* — *Sentry post*

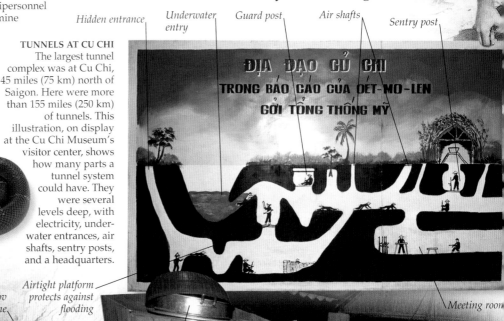

ĐỊA ĐẠO CỦ CHI
TRONG BÁO CÁO CỦA ĐỆT-MO-LEN
GỞI TỔNG THỐNG MỸ

Meeting room

Rice cooker

SKS Simonov carbine

Airtight platform protects against flooding

ON GUARD
A VC sentry waiting underground is alert for possible enemy discovery of his tunnel. The entrance to a tunnel is at right.

Cover over food keeps out bugs and rodents

Wood stoves

Wash bucket

UNDERGROUND KITCHEN
The cooking area of a tunnel mess hall was vented by shafts that sent smoke in many directions to make it unseen aboveground. Some VC lived underground for months at a time and seldom saw sunlight. They would suddenly come out to make an attack and just as suddenly vanish into the tunnels before their enemies recovered.

RETURNING TUNNEL RAT

A U.S. soldier is pulled out of a tunnel he has just searched. In general, Americans were physically larger than Vietnamese and had trouble squeezing through the narrow tunnels. This man wears a gas mask and goggles against tear gas he threw into the tunnel before entering.

Flak jacket

Gas mask

Flashlight

Tunnel rats

"Tunnel rats" were a special breed of soldier who took on one of the most dangerous and frightening duties of the war. At first termed "tunnel runners," they were extremely courageous and daring. They risked their lives by crawling alone into unexplored VC tunnels to find if they led to major networks or supply centers. With only a pistol, knife, and flashlight, they squirmed through twisting, dark tunnels. They might meet a waiting enemy sentry or run into a hidden booby trap—or might find nothing at all.

Pull-ring

GAS AND GAS MASK

Before entering a tunnel, a tunnel rat often tossed in a tear-gas canister. He hoped any enemy guards in there would be sickened and forced away by the nauseating gas. Wearing a gas mask so he could breathe, the soldier then crawled into the tunnel.

GAS
CN-DM

PB-2-68

Handle

Tear gas

Air filter

Tear gas mask

Strap

Special non-rolling design

Belt clip

.45 caliber bullet

TUNNEL RAT GEAR

The .45 pistol was the tunnel rat's most potent weapon, but he also carried a "Ka-Bar" combat knife. There were instances of men encountering enemies in the tunnels, and deadly shootouts resulted. Since tunnels were designed with many turns, bullets traveled only short distances before hitting a wall.

.45 pistol

Bullet and magazine

Flashlight

Hilt

Handle

Ka-Bar knife

Ka-Bar sheath

NO ROOM TO SPARE

A 173rd Airborne Division engineer squats with knife and pistol in a tunnel 15 feet (4.6 m) below the surface. He is in the "Iron Triangle" region, a VC stronghold north of Saigon. His unit is searching for VC caches of food and ammunition.

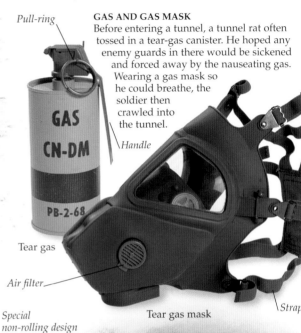

Khe Sanh and Tet

YEAR OF THE MONKEY
The Vietnamese give each year a Chinese zodiac animal symbol, such as a snake or horse, and 1968 was the Year of the Monkey. According to the zodiac, the monkey is a creature that often desires revenge.

ON JANUARY 21, 1968, the Communists surprised the U.S. Marine base camp of Khe Sanh with a storm of artillery fire. This opened General Giap's long-planned offensive that erupted all over South Vietnam on January 30. The assaults began during the Vietnamese New Year, known as "Tet," when half the ARVN troops were home on leave. The Tet Offensive struck more than 100 cities and towns, even the center of Saigon. Fighting raged for four weeks, inflicting heavy losses on the Communists, who were defeated. Yet Americans now knew the war had no end in sight.

TET OFFENSIVE
Bases and government buildings across South Vietnam were attacked during Tet. Hué and Saigon came under the fiercest assaults.

Khe Sanh

Khe Sanh's 6,000 Marines and ARVN troops blocked enemy supply routes from Laos. The Communist siege of the base in early 1968 intended to draw other Allied forces away from the cities, which were soon attacked. Thousands of U.S. and Allied troops battled to get through to the base, which gallantly held out for 77 days before being relieved.

LBJ STUDIES KHE SANH
President Johnson and advisors examine a scale model of besieged Khe Sanh. LBJ believed Giap wanted to turn Khe Sanh into another Dien Bien Phu. Such a defeat would force the United States to withdraw, as the French had in 1954. For two-and-a-half months, Americans anxiously followed the course of the siege.

U.S. M-101 howitzer

KHE SANH ARTILLERY
American gunners at Khe Sanh reply to enemy artillery fire with their own bombardment. Marines and South Vietnamese allies fought hand to hand to drive off enemy infantry attacks. Each week, the defenders were hit with 2,500 rounds of Communist artillery, mortars, and rockets.

EXPLOSION AT KHE SANH
Marines duck as an ammunition storage pit takes a direct hit. Like Dien Bien Phu, Khe Sanh was surrounded by hills with Communist gun positions. The Americans, however, had overwhelming air power that blasted those guns. Also, helicopters braved hostile fire, bringing in supplies and evacuating wounded. Relief forces fought their way through on April 8, finally ending the siege.

Saigon

The most important struggle of the Tet Offensive was the battle for Saigon, South Vietnam's capital city. A team of 19 VC guerrillas broke into the U.S. embassy compound and fought for several hours before being wiped out. The main event was the assault on MACV headquarters at Tan Son Nhut airfield. U.S. and Allied forces led by General Frederick Weyand fought off every VC attack, defeating the enemy by February 5.

FREDERICK C. WEYAND (b. 1916)
As commander of II Field Force (which defended Saigon), General Weyand received warnings of a coming major assault. He pulled his forces closer to Saigon to be ready. Weyand's success during Tet earned him eventual promotion to overall command in Vietnam.

South Vietnamese flag

Hué

Most Tet fighting ended in a few days, but the battle for Hué lasted until March 2. Part of this ancient city had been the capital of imperial Vietnam. Fighting destroyed much of Hué and its Imperial Citadel, or fortress. Although the Communists lost Tet, they won a political victory: many more Americans opposed the war. Tet was the turning point of the Vietnam conflict, which increasingly favored the Communists.

SAIGON RECOVERS FROM TET
Saigon had seen little violence before Tet. Afterward, residents had to pick their way through endless rubble to search for victims and clean up their homes.

VIET CONG IN HUÉ
As the battle rages, a VC radio operator sends messages to Communist troops in Hué. The radioman is in Hué's Imperial Citadel, which saw fierce fighting.

VIETNAMESE RANGER
35   BN

ARVN
Ranger patch

ARVN RETAKE CITADEL
Weary South Vietnamese troops have planted their flag on a tower of Hué's Citadel, shattered by a month of conflict. U.S. and ARVN forces attacked VC and NVA fighters holding the walled fortress, and Allied warplanes and naval gunfire blasted enemy-occupied buildings.

AFTER THE BATTLE
Members of the U.S. Fifth Marine Regiment patrol a war-littered street in Hué. These troops reinforced Allied units and fought for three brutal weeks to recapture the city. The destroyed Imperial Citadel is in the background.

Peace symbol

"V" peace sign

The antiwar movement

BY 1965, MANY AMERICANS OPPOSED their government's involvement in Vietnam. That year, more than 20,000 antiwar demonstrators marched in Washington, D.C. At first, the war's supporters and opponents joined in "teach-ins" to debate their positions peacefully. As the war worsened, opposition increased and demonstrations grew in size and anger. Hundreds of thousands gathered at major protests, where famous performers and political leaders spoke out against the war. President Johnson was so troubled by the widespread antiwar movement that he chose not to run in 1968. Hostility caused clashes between Americans for and against the war. In 1970, several college students were killed when soldiers in Ohio and police in Mississippi shot protesters.

PEACE SIGNS
The peace symbol, top, appeared in early demonstrations against nuclear weapons. The *V* for victory became a sign of unity for antiwar Democrats in 1968.

A VOICE FOR PEACE
Folksinger Joan Baez joined leading antiwar musicians such as Pete Seeger, Phil Ochs, Bob Dylan, and the group Peter, Paul and Mary to entertain at peace demonstrations.

RESPECTED LEADERS
Famous baby doctor and author Benjamin Spock, far left, marches with civil rights champion Dr. Martin Luther King Jr., near left, at a 1967 peace rally in Chicago. They led 5,000 people in the protest march, demanding an end to the Vietnam War. The influence of such highly regarded leaders convinced many Americans to oppose the war.

1969 Moratorium Against the War button

moratorium

PROFESSIONAL GROUPS

FLOWERS INSTEAD OF BULLETS
In one of the most famous photographs of the antiwar movement, a demonstrator places carnations in the barrels of military police rifles. This incident occurred during a 1967 demonstration by more than 100,000 protesters at the Pentagon, headquarters of the Defense Department in Washington.

Tear gas canister

Tear gas mask

Launcher for tear gas canister

GAS, THEN BULLETS
Ohio national guardsmen fire tear gas at Kent State University demonstrators in May 1970. Troops also fired bullets that killed four students and wounded others. Some casualties were not protesters, but just students walking to class. The shootings sparked a nationwide student strike, closing hundreds of campuses. Two students at Jackson State College in Mississippi were also shot and killed, by police, later that month.

FIGHTING BACK
A protester in Berkeley, California, hurls a tear gas canister back at police who had fired it, in 1970. Tear gas briefly burned the eyes and throat and forced most demonstrators to retreat.

U.S. Capitol Building

North Vietnamese flag

Vietnam Veterans Against the War symbol

MARCH FOR A MORATORIUM ON THE WAR
In November 1969, huge demonstrations occurred all across America, urging an immediate moratorium—a temporary halt in the fighting. One march filled Pennsylvania Avenue, near the Capitol Building in Washington. Signs called for U.S. troops in Vietnam to get "Out Now" and for the release of jailed antiwar activists. The main demonstrations were mostly peaceful, but afterward some protesters battled with police.

VIETNAM VETERANS AGAINST THE WAR
Among the strongest opponents of the Vietnam conflict were soldiers who had served over there and considered the war wrong. Their main organization was Vietnam Veterans Against the War, shown marching in Miami Beach in 1972. Many antiwar veterans threw away their medals in protest.

Silver Star

Dove of peace

McGovern campaign button

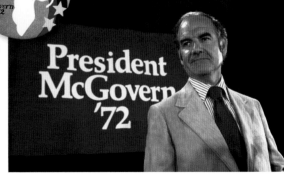

PEACE CANDIDATE
The Democratic Party chose Senator George McGovern of South Dakota to run against President Nixon in 1972. McGovern was himself a decorated World War II bomber pilot and was highly regarded in Congress. Yet he could not unify Democrat voters behind his promises to end the war and cut defense spending. Nixon won a landslide victory.

U.S. withdrawal begins

North Vietnamese flag

In 1969, President Nixon pressed the military for "Vietnamization" of the conflict. This meant improved training and arming of South Vietnam's military, which was to take a larger role in defending the country. It also involved the withdrawal of U.S. forces, which numbered 543,000 by that spring—the largest amount of the war. ARVN soldiers had shown they could fight well if led by good commanders. Unfortunately, too many of their top officers—including President Nguyen Van Thieu, overall commander—lacked military ability. On the other hand, ARVN forces led by able officers showed steady improvement during 1969. Still, it would be years before the Americans could be completely replaced. Nixon hoped to limit U.S. casualties, but bloody battles continued. Many U.S. soldiers became angry with the Nixon administration for sending them into action while the military was gradually leaving Vietnam.

RVN flag

A VICTORY
South Vietnamese security forces fighting alongside the ARVN proudly show off a captured North Vietnamese flag. Communist flags and a cache of VC arms and munitions were taken during counter-insurgency operations near the DMZ.

CREIGHTON ABRAMS
General Abrams (1914–1974) took command of MACV in 1968, replacing General Westmoreland. Abrams was ordered to end large-scale U.S. operations and supervise "Vietnamization" of the war.

HOMEWARD BOUND
Troops of the 9th Infantry Division board a Chinook helicopter to begin their journey back to the United States. They were part of a 25,000-strong troop withdrawal that began in June 1969.

General Thi   President Thieu

A CHEST FULL OF MEDALS
South Vietnamese president Thieu pins another medal on a well-decorated officer. Thieu is joined by General Lam Quang Thi (b. 1932), commander of the National Military Academy. Thieu was criticized for making many bad military decisions. He and Thi led the effort to build up their forces during Vietnamization.

NGO QUANG TRUONG
General Truong (b. 1929) shows captured enemy weapons to visiting U.S. secretary of state William P. Rogers. A top ARVN commander, Truong was highly regarded by U.S. officers as well as by his own troops.

ARVN TROOPS ON PATROL
South Vietnamese Marines gather at a village in the Mekong Delta on a mission to cut a VC supply route. As U.S. troops were withdrawing, ARVN forces assumed more patrol and reconnaissance duties. The best South Vietnamese troops proved themselves to be effective soldiers. To build a larger military, the government began drafting men between the ages of 17 and 43.

Dragon

Leopard

ARVN PATCHES
These shoulder patches were worn by hard-hitting South Vietnamese Special Forces units. The Black Dragons attacked the Ho Chi Minh Trail in Laos and Cambodia. The Yellow Leopards were daring paratroopers.

Yellow Leopard patch   Black Dragon patch

Hamburger Hill

On May 10, 1969, heliborne troopers of the 101st Airborne assaulted NVA forces dug in on top of Ap Bia Mountain, near the Laotian border. The military labeled this peak Hill 937. A savage battle raged for ten days, costing 46 American deaths and 400 wounded. Troopers named the mountain "Hamburger Hill," because they felt they had been thrown into a meat grinder. Joined by ARVN troops, they captured Ap Bia but soon were ordered to abandon it. Many Americans, especially soldiers, believed the losses had been for nothing. Nixon now ordered General Abrams to avoid further engagements that would result in heavy U.S. casualties. Hamburger Hill was the last major battle fought by American troops in the Vietnam War.

REINFORCEMENTS LANDING
Paratroopers jump down from a helicopter to join the battle for 3,000-foot (1,000-m) Ap Bia Mountain. The peak dominated the strategic A Shau Valley, where NVA forces operated in large numbers. This valley was a route for Communist troops and supplies to penetrate the Central Highlands region.

MEDICS AID THE WOUNDED
American and ARVN "walking wounded" make their way down Ap Bia Mountain with the help of medics. The ten-day fight for "Hamburger Hill" has just ended after the capture of the last NVA positions. These soldiers pass other wounded, who soon will be taken to a rear area for treatment. Many will fly out by medevac helicopters, but those only slightly injured will return to their units.

NORTH VIETNAM

CHINA

NVA bases and supply routes

DMZ

LAOS

CAMBODIA

SOUTH VIETNAM

Quang Tri
Hué

Kontum
Pleiku

Central Highlands

An Loc

Tay Ninh

Saigon

Mekong River

South China Sea

N
W E
S

✱ Battle sites

Areas lost by S. Vietnam in 1972

NVA Eastertide Offensive

KEY BATTLES OF 1972
Giap's March 30 offensive surprised ARVN defenders, who fought hard as they fell back. The invasion brought on major struggles at Kontum, Quang Tri, and An Loc. The Communists were defeated by September.

Last air assaults

THROUGH 1970, U.S. FORCES steadily withdrew, but U.S. air power continued to support the South Vietnamese. President Nixon ordered bombing raids against Communist positions in Cambodia, which further angered antiwar activists at home. Brief incursions (invasions) by U.S. and ARVN forces struck Communist bases in Cambodia. Early in 1971, ARVN troops entered Laos, but were routed with severe loss. By 1972, there were no more American offensive operations. Only 70,000 U.S. troops remained in Vietnam. In February, President Nixon visited China and opened diplomatic relations with Premier Zhou En-lai's government. That March, General Giap sent 125,000 troops on the attack, backed by tanks and artillery. ARVN units fell back until a heavy U.S. bombing campaign blunted the invasion. Code-named "Linebacker," the air campaign also struck strategic targets in North Vietnam. Then the ARVN counterattacked, pushing back the Communists. Giap's bold assault, known as the Spring—or Easter—Offensive, was soundly defeated.

NIXON AND ZHOU TOAST
When Nixon visited Beijing, Vietnamese Communists worried he would make a deal to withdraw Chinese support from Hanoi. They opposed any call for peace that would leave Vietnam divided.

ADVANCING NVA SOLDIERS
Camouflaged NVA troops trudge along a trail in Cambodia, heading for South Vietnam. They are on the way to join the Spring Offensive of early 1972.

AWAITING A LIFT
South Vietnamese airborne troops near the town of An Loc in April 1972 prepare for helicopter transport. An Loc was between the Communists and their objective—the capital city of Saigon, about 75 miles (120 km) away.

PREPARING TO FIRE
An NVA soldier loads a shell into a mortar—one of the main Communist weapons. Most mortars could be carried into action by two soldiers, while other troops brought up the ammunition.

JAMES F. HOLLINGSWORTH
General Hollingsworth (b. 1918) planned the air attacks that helped defeat NVA assaults at An Loc. Hollingsworth was serving as the senior military advisor to the ARVN corps defending Saigon.

Wright brothers' plane

AIRCRAFT CARRIER CREWMAN PATCH
The USS *Kitty Hawk* was one of the Navy carriers whose jets helped stem the Communist Spring Offensive. The carrier was named in honor of the North Carolina site where the Wright brothers first flew.

500-lb bomb

LOADING BOMBS
Navy crewmen on the carrier USS *Constellation* load fighter-bombers with 500-lb (230 kg) bombs for the Linebacker campaign. This carrier was one of five Navy "flattops" stationed off Vietnam. The air campaign also dropped mines into North Vietnamese harbors. These mines threatened commercial shipping carrying supplies for Hanoi's war effort. Linebacker would be followed by a second bombing campaign known as Linebacker II (see pages 56–57).

Shark-tooth decoration

Cobra helicopter crewman's patch

Rockets

COBRA HELICOPTER
Cobra attack helicopters such as this Air Cav gunship were among the best weapons employed in the Linebacker air campaign. The rocket-armed Cobra was an especially effective tank-destroyer during the Spring Offensive of 1972. More than 200 Soviet-made tanks led the offensive, but they were no match for Cobras. By mid-May, Cobras firing antitank rockets had blunted a major armored offensive at Kontum in central Vietnam.

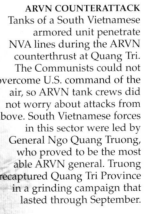

ARVN COUNTERATTACK
Tanks of a South Vietnamese armored unit penetrate NVA lines during the ARVN counterthrust at Quang Tri. The Communists could not overcome U.S. command of the air, so ARVN tank crews did not worry about attacks from above. South Vietnamese forces in this sector were led by General Ngo Quang Truong, who proved to be the most able ARVN general. Truong recaptured Quang Tri Province in a grinding campaign that lasted through September.

ANTITANK WEAPON
The shoulder-fired LAW (light antitank weapon) was crucial in the ARVN's battle with NVA tanks. The LAW launched 66-mm rockets that could knock out Soviet-made armor.

The Christmas Bombing

As the 1972 Communist offensive continued, peace talks were under way in Paris. Henry Kissinger (b. 1923)—a close advisor to Nixon—was head of the American delegation. In October, Kissinger announced an agreement was at hand, and Nixon called off the air campaign. Then it turned out that the Vietnamese Communists refused the U.S. condition that Vietnam remain divided. When the talks broke down, Nixon decided to bomb North Vietnam into accepting a cease-fire agreement. He launched Linebacker II, bombarding North Vietnam from December 18–30. Termed the "Christmas Bombing," this was the heaviest bombing of the war. It ruined the nation's industrial capacity and transportation system and forced the Communists to accept a cease-fire.

AIR FORCE PATCH
The 1972 buildup of U.S. heavy bombers in the Pacific was code-named "Operation Bullet Shot." More than 12,000 personnel and 150 B-52s were readied at Andersen Air Force Base in Guam. From Guam, the high-altitude B-52s flew approximately 3,000 miles (4,800 km) each way to attack North Vietnam.

HEROISM MEDAL
The Distinguished Flying Cross (DFC) is awarded for heroism in flight, both in combat or noncombat. Two DFCs were awarded during the Linebacker II campaign.

Identification number

BOMBS AWAY!
A "string" of 750-pound (340 kg) bombs falls from a B-52D Stratofortress over Vietnam. Air Force and Navy warplanes pounded the cities of Hanoi and Haiphong with 20,000 tons of bombs. The bombing was so massive that the warplanes soon found few remaining targets worth attacking.

Weaving leaves and brush together

70162

B-52 WING PATCH
The 449th Bombardment Wing flew B-52s over Southeast Asia. They also flew KC-135 tanker aircraft, which provided mid-air refueling services.

Black underside for camouflage in night bombing

ANTIAIRCRAFT DEFENSES
North Vietnamese militia load an antiaircraft gun in December 1972. U.S. fixed-wing aircraft losses numbered 26 during Linebacker II—15 of these were B-52s. Antiaircraft artillery and MiG fighters shot down three planes each, SAMs downed 17, and three crashed for unknown reasons. By the campaign's end, the North's air defenses had run out of ammunition or had been destroyed.

U.S. AIRCRAFT DOWN
North Vietnamese women salvage parts from the wreckage of an F-111 fighter-bomber. The Air Force lost two such aircraft in Linebacker II. Of the 26 planes lost, 20 were Air Force (which also lost a helicopter) and 6 were Navy.

Palm leaves

CONCEALING A BRIDGE
North Vietnamese villagers camouflage a bridge with brush and leaves. This made it difficult for U.S. warplanes to discover from above. Air attacks targeted bridges to cut transportation links. Camouflage protected the small bridges that were essential to the movement of the people. Large bridges, however, were easy targets for U.S. bombers. The Vietnamese had fought for years against enemies who had control of the air.

Camouflage

Clearing wood debris

LE DUAN (1907–1986)
Younger leaders such as Le Duan gained power with the 1969 death of Ho Chi Minh. A high official in the Communist Party, Le Duan pushed for Vietnam's reunification. He favored military action over any agreement that left Vietnam divided. Le Duan was willing to let the peace talks collapse if unsatisfactory terms were offered.

HOSPITAL IN RUINS
Doctors and nurses pick their way through the rubble of a Hanoi hospital destroyed by the Christmas Bombing. They are looking for supplies that can be saved. U.S. airmen tried to avoid damaging hospitals and schools, but high-altitude bombing was not accurate enough to prevent such destruction.

Paris Peace Accords

As U.S. air raids hammered North Vietnam in December 1972, Communist delegates to the Paris peace talks agreed to a cease-fire. On January 27, 1973, the Paris Peace Accords were signed by the United States, North Vietnam, South Vietnam, and the Viet Cong. The accords provided for a cease-fire, with the United States withdrawing from Vietnam. Vietnamese troops in the field would hold their present positions while their leaders consulted on the future. North Vietnam's top delegate, Le Duc Tho (1910–1990), and Kissinger were awarded the Nobel Prize for Peace in 1973. Tho declined to accept, however, saying the accords did not guarantee a lasting peace. He proved right, as large-scale warfare began again in 1975.

Round conference table

DELEGATES IN PARIS
Henry Kissinger, left, converses with North Vietnam's Le Duc Tho through an interpreter, center. These diplomats were heads of their delegations to the peace talks. They first began secret negotiations in 1970. Kissinger developed Nixon's Vietnamization policy of withdrawing U.S. troops from Vietnam. Le Duc Tho was determined to reunify Vietnam, even at a high cost to his people.

DISCUSSING PEACE TERMS
Paris peace talks delegates gather at a round table, so no country could claim the "head of the table" and be symbolically in charge. A cease-fire was accepted on January 27, 1973. Secretary of State William P. Rogers signed for the United States.

Le Duc Tho

MADAME BINH
Madame Nguyen Thi Binh (b. 1927) signs the cease-fire agreement in Paris for the National Liberation Front and Viet Cong. Madame Binh was one of the most important NLF leaders. Throughout the Paris negotiations, the dignified Madame Binh was often seen on U.S. television as the public face of the NLF.

Prisoners of war

MORE THAN 660 U.S. SERVICEMEN were taken prisoners of war (POWs). A few were held as long as nine years, and some escaped. Approximately 470 were held in North Vietnam—many were abused, others tortured. Another 260 were in jungle detention camps in South Vietnam, Laos, and Cambodia. Thousands of Communists were captured, but the ARVN routinely killed captives instead of imprisoning them. The Paris peace negotiators agreed to release all POWs when the American military left Vietnam. In early 1973, Operation Homecoming airlifted former U.S. POWs back to the United States. By March, 591 POWs had returned. Nixon soon assured the nation that everyone was freed, but some 2,400 men missing in action (MIA) still remain unaccounted for.

POW/MIA FLAG
The National League of POW/MIA Families designed this flag to remember Vietnam War prisoners and the missing. It is the only flag other than the Stars and Stripes to be displayed in the Capitol Rotunda in Washington, D.C., or to fly over the White House.

POW/MIA BRACELET
As a remembrance, Americans wore silver bracelets inscribed with the names of POWs or MIAs and the dates of their capture or disappearance.

A NURSE'S COMFORT
For three months, Navy nurse Lt. Patricia Anderson wore a bracelet with the name of Lt. Charles Norris. When he was released, she helped nurse him back to health.

PARADE OF PRISONERS
American POWs are marched under military guard through the streets of Hanoi in 1966. They were filmed for propaganda purposes, and their images broadcast around the world. American POWs were mostly Air Force and Navy fliers, captured when their planes were shot down. During the war, 30 American POWs managed to escape.

Nurse Patricia Anderson

FIRST TASTE OF FREEDOM
American POWs under North Vietnamese guard disembark from a bus on their way to a Hanoi airport in early 1973. They will take a flight to freedom, with their first stop in the Philippines. The release was arranged at the Paris peace talks. Operation Homecoming transported hundreds of former POWs back to the United States, where they were awarded special POW medals.

POW medal

Communist POWs

There is no accurate estimate of the thousands of Communist fighters and sympathizers imprisoned during the war. NVA and VC captives were sent to POW camps in South Vietnam. On the way, they were usually interrogated, often brutally—especially if taken by the ARVN. In camp, they were classified by rank, assigned serial numbers, fingerprinted, and photographed. Also, they were issued clothing, toilet articles, and mess gear. The terms of the Paris Peace Accords arranged for an exchange of prisoners between the Communists and the United States.

Communist star

Hands breaking free from chains

NVA POW medal

POW medal

Victory medal

FORMER NVA POW
The Communists honored their own former POWs, as seen in this photograph of Nguyen Huu Thanh. Once an American captive, Thanh wears the NVA's POW medal pinned to his shirt pocket.

DREARY ACCOMMODATIONS
American POWs are seen at the "Hanoi Hilton," as they nicknamed their prison. One prisoner has been permitted to talk with others who are locked in their cells.

A JOYFUL WELCOME
Returning Air Force colonel Robert L. Stirm hurries to the arms of his family as they greet him at Travis Air Force Base in California in March 1973. Stirm had been a prisoner of war for more than five years.

A SURVIVOR AND CAPTIVE
A soldier of the NVA 304th Division sits, bound and battle-shocked, under the watchful eye of a trooper from the 1st Air Cavalry Division. The prisoner was taken during fighting in the Ia Drang Valley of the Central Highlands, which saw heavy NVA losses.

Binding rope

TAKING IN SUSPECTS
A U.S. officer, pistol in hand, pushes along suspected members of the Viet Cong being brought in for interrogation. The prisoners are bound with a rope to keep them from trying to run away. The youthfulness of the captives is typical of many South Vietnamese who seemed to be farmers but were actually guerrillas.

The fall of Saigon

IN 1973, THE UNITED STATES promised to strike back at the Communists if they resumed attacking South Vietnam. This promise was not kept. That same year, Congress cut off funds for U.S. military involvement in Southeast Asia. Later, Congress cut military aid to the Saigon government. When the NVA invaded the RVN province of Phuoc Long in December 1974, President Gerald Ford could do nothing in response. The Communist offensive had begun. The South Vietnamese knew they had been abandoned by America—their morale was crushed. The NVA's final campaign went into full swing in March 1975. Now, the NVA were better armed than the ARVN. In a lightning war, the NVA swept through South Vietnam, capturing Saigon in April. This campaign ended almost 30 years of continuous fighting in Vietnam.

VAN TIEN DUNG (1917–2002)
General Dung had been the NVA commander in chief since 1953 and fought at Dien Bien Phu. In 1975, he personally led the final campaign that broke through ARVN defenses in the Central Highlands and charged on to Saigon.

LOOKING FOR A SAFE PLACE
ARVN soldiers help fleeing villagers cross a bamboo footbridge over an irrigation ditch. NVA and VC forces are approaching this area, 50 miles (80 km) northwest of Saigon. Hordes of frightened South Vietnamese left their homes to escape the fighting. Many ran out of food and water and had no shelter; thousands died along the way. Many soldiers left their military units to rejoin their families attempting to get away from the invading Communists.

THE STRUGGLE TO ESCAPE
Frightened Saigon residents wave identification documents as they try to board a U.S. Embassy bus on April 24, 1975. They are desperate for transportation to the airport and hope to be flown out of the country. Those who worked for the government or the Americans were in danger of punishment by NVA forces surrounding the city.

LAST-MINUTE EVACUATION
A U.S. helicopter loads passengers from a rooftop helipad near the U.S. Embassy on April 29. By late on April 30, helicopters had evacuated more than 3,000 Americans, South Vietnamese, and other foreign nationals from the embassy compound. On that day, South Vietnam's government surrendered. Another 400 persons trying to escape Saigon were left behind at the embassy as Communist forces entered the city.

FINAL CAMPAIGN

The NVA offensive of March–April 1975 was named the "Ho Chi Minh Campaign." ARVN troops fought hard, although they were attacked on all sides. They made gallant stands even without U.S. air power to support them. The ARVN inflicted heavy casualties on the NVA, but were wiped out in less than two months.

LAOS
DMZ
Hué
Da Nang
SOUTH VIETNAM
CAMBODIA
Central Highlands
Ban Me Thuot
Phuoc Long
Phnom Penh
Cam Ranh Bay
Xuan Loc
Saigon
Mekong River
South China Sea

— Final NVA campaign March–April 1975
★ South Vietnamese cities and provinces captured by the NVA

CRASHING THE PALACE GATES

A tank sporting an NVA flag rumbles into the South Vietnamese presidential palace compound on April 30, 1975. Until now, infantry and guerrillas had done most of the Communist fighting, but the final offensive was by a modern mechanized army. The well-equipped NVA assaults were spearheaded by heavy armor.

VICTORY MEDAL

North Vietnam awarded its soldiers this Victory Order and Decoration for fighting South Vietnam, the United States, and their allies. The same medal was first awarded in the 1950s for fighting the French.

THE WAKE OF DEFEAT

Thousands of ARVN soldiers threw away their uniforms, helmets, and combat boots as they tried to escape from Saigon on April 30, 1975. Afraid of being made prisoners of war, they dressed as civilians and tried to mix with refugees. This photograph of a littered road was taken from a car carrying victorious Communists into the city.

REJOICING IN HANOI

Thousands of North Vietnamese marchers gather in Hanoi in May 1975. They carry signs and banners and pictures of Ho Chi Minh as they rally in front of Hanoi's opera house. Smartly turned-out military units join the celebration, which marked the end of a century-long struggle for Vietnamese independence.

Aftermath

THE VIETNAM WAR COST the lives of more than 58,000 Americans, with more than 153,000 seriously wounded. One million Vietnamese combatants and four million civilians were killed. The number of Vietnamese wounded is unknown. The new Socialist Republic of Vietnam was a nation shattered by war, and bitterness remained between Communists and noncommunists. Hundreds of thousands of former RVN officials and officers were imprisoned. Many people tried to escape to other countries, especially to the United States. Most left in small, overcrowded boats. As Vietnam struggled to recover, its population grew from 49 million in 1976 to 82.6 million by 2004. Three-fourths of the people live in rural areas, and most work in agriculture. Vietnam is modernizing, but it lags behind other, more progressive Asian nations.

NATIONALIST POSTER
Hanoi became Vietnam's capital, and Saigon was renamed Ho Chi Minh City—where this poster was seen in 1980. It shows the dove of peace over a united Vietnam guarded by a soldier.

IN A MONASTERY
This Buddhist monk is a former ARVN soldier who devoted himself to a religious life. The Communist government restricts Buddhism and has taken over Buddhist hospitals, schools, and other institutions. Vietnam's Buddhists believe only faith and compassion can help heal their country.

REMEMBERING THE FALLEN
Visitors to a cemetery honor fallen NVA soldiers during the Vietnamese New Year in 1985. Burning incense sticks are placed beside graves as a way of honoring the dead. ARVN cemeteries are usually neglected, however, are considered the graves of enemies of the state.

MOTHERS' MEDAL
The sacrifices of North Vietnam's wartime mothers were recognized by this 1994 medal, accompanied by the title "Hero Mother."

A TIME OF PEACE
In 2003, young Vietnamese newlyweds pose before a statue of Ho Chi Minh, in Ho Chi Minh City. The statue was erected after the war. The former Saigon, population 7 million, is Vietnam's largest city.

The boat people

As Saigon fell, modern history's largest mass flight of refugees by sea began. Fearing the Communists, hundreds of thousands of South Vietnamese fled in small vessels. Termed "boat people," they made long, dangerous journeys to other countries in the region. Many drowned at sea. Some families spent their life savings to send their children off in a boat. They hoped their children could make a new start and help the rest of the family follow later. More than a million refugees from the conflict in Indochina eventually settled in the United States.

RESCUED
Fleeing the Communists, these South Vietnamese boat people have been rescued from a leaking vessel in the South China Sea. They are mainly former government officials or soldiers and their families. The next waves of boat people would be Vietnamese farmers and laborers seeking better economic conditions elsewhere.

IN HONG KONG HARBOR
Vietnamese refugees huddle on an overcrowded boat in Hong Kong harbor in 1979. In this year, almost 69,000 boat people reached Hong Kong, making a 1,000-mile (1,600 km) journey. Boat people included many Amerasians—the children of Vietnamese women and U.S. military personnel.

Overloaded vessel is dangerously low in water

Vietnam veterans

Allied forces' veterans often faced resentment when they returned home. Many people believed they had lost the war and had not been dedicated enough. Others believed they had fought in an unjust war. At first, some older veterans' groups in the United States did not want to accept Vietnam veterans as members. In time it became clear how well Allied servicemen and women had done their duty. Then Vietnam veterans were given the respect they had earned serving their country in extremely difficult conditions. Approximately 2.64 million U.S. personnel served within the borders of South Vietnam from January 1960 to March 1973. Of this total, almost 1.6 million fought in combat, provided combat support, or were exposed to attack.

Fuse (or trigger)

LAND MINES
Thousands of land mines like this Soviet-made antitank mine remain uncleared in Vietnam. By 2004, approximately 40,000 Vietnamese had died and thousands more had been injured by land mines left after the fighting stopped.

VETERAN'S BUCKLE
This belt buckle commemorates Australian service in Vietnam.

WRITTEN IN STONE
An American Vietnam veteran touches "The Wall," a memorial bearing the names of U.S. dead from the war. This national memorial in Washington, D.C., was dedicated in 1981 (see pages 68–69).

LIFE GOES ON
A farmer's elephant lumbers by a rusting tank more than ten years after war's end. By 1985 this abandoned tank had not been removed from its resting place in Quang Tri Province. The modern war machine is useless, but the traditional beast of burden is still at work in Vietnam's countryside. Vietnam had an enormous task clearing away ruined military equipment after the conflict.

U.S. VETERANS
Vietnam War veterans parade past saluting spectators during 1993 Veterans Day events at the national Vietnam Veterans Memorial in Washington, D.C. More than 8.2 million veterans served in the U.S. military, around the world, during the Vietnam era. They accounted for more than one-third of all U.S. veterans in 2004 and were the largest single group of living veterans from America's wars.

Did you know?

FASCINATING FACTS

One third of the top National Liberation Front (NLF) political officers were women. Among the most important was Nguyen Thi Binh, chief representative of the NLF at the Paris peace talks. Many of these women entered the Vietnamese government after the war.

"Mining" warplanes for precious metals could be profitable. As much as $5,000 worth of gold, silver, and platinum could be found in the instruments and gear of an American warplane.

U.S. soldiers often painted an "Ace Of Death" playing card symbol on their vehicles. It was also carried by soldiers, who used it to frighten superstitious Vietnamese. The symbol was considered bad luck in Vietnam.

Death's Head playing card

U.S. soldiers were supposed to destroy any letters they received. So, if a soldier were captured, the enemy would not be able to read his letters and find out personal information. Most troops kept their letters, however, and reread them often.

NVA officers in the field wore no distinguishing badge of rank. Instead, they carried pens to show they were officers. The pen was often secured with a short string and a safety pin and kept in a shirt pocket.

North Vietnamese officer's pen

In the early 1970s, the ARVN captured so many AK-47 assault rifles from the NVA that they gave away thousands to other Southeast Asian armies.

Documents that secretly circulated among Communist commanders and officials in South Vietnam were often stamped with symbols known only to those handling the papers.

An estimated 50,000 Vietnamese children were fathered by American servicemen during the Vietnam War. The men returned home, leaving mothers and children behind. These "Amerasian" children were discriminated against by the Vietnamese government, which considered them legally Americans. Some were taken to the United States for adoption, but most remained social outcasts in Vietnam.

The $8.4 million collected to erect the Vietnam Veterans Memorial in Washington, D.C., included small contributions from more than 275,000 individuals.

The French author Bernard B. Fall was the leading authority on the Indochina conflict. U.S. commander William C. Westmoreland studied Fall's works closely. A former French soldier, Fall attended college in the United States, where he became a college professor at Howard University in Washington, D.C. His works, such as *Street Without Joy*, chronicled the First Indochina War. Fall was killed by a land mine in Vietnam in 1967.

NVA stamp for official documents

Soldiers on patrol were told not to use anything with a fragrance, such as soap, cologne, or shampoo. VC might detect these odors in the jungle and know U.S. troops were nearby.

Of the 7,484 U.S. women who served in Vietnam, 6,250—or 83.5 percent—were nurses. Ten women serving in the military died, as did 56 civilians—including missionaries, nurses, and journalists. In a single tragedy, 37 of these civilian women died in a plane crash while escorting Vietnamese Amerasian orphans being flown out of the country in April 1975.

Just as U.S. troops had well-known performers come to entertain them, the NVA and VC troops had their own entertainers. Performances were sometimes given in specially built underground theater spaces in tunnels.

These girls, seen in Ho Chi Minh City, have Vietnamese mothers and American fathers.

Communist performers entertain North Vietnamese troops.

QUESTIONS AND ANSWERS

Q Ever hear of a "flying banana"?

A This was the nickname given to a series of large military transport helicopters that were banana-shaped. The powerful H-21 Shawnee has rotors "in tandem"— one at the front and a smaller rotor at the back.

H-21 Shawnee transport helicopter

Q Was the U.S. K-9 Corps important in the war?

A Yes, the K-9 (for "canine," meaning "dog") Corps is the unit that trains dogs for various military duties. U.S. troops used German shepherds as sentry dogs and to sniff out booby traps or find the disturbed soil of hidden VC tunnels. Scout dogs were so valuable that enemy mortars specifically targeted dog shelters for destruction.

Q What was the "domino theory"?

A This theory said that if South Vietnam fell to the Communists, then other Southeast Asian nations would fall— just as a row of dominoes standing on end can knock each other down.

Q When is the worst weather in Vietnam?

A Monsoon season has endless rain. There are summer and winter monsoons, depending on the region. Soldiers' clothing never dried, causing boils, disease, and infection from parasites.

Q How educated were U.S. soldiers in Vietnam?

A The average education level of lower ranks (non-officers) in Vietnam was 13 years. This is equal to having one year of college. Of those who volunteered, 79 percent had high school diplomas.

Montagnards sometimes gave U.S. soldiers friendship bracelets and flutes.

Q Were any Vietnamese ethnic groups U.S. allies?

A Yes, the Montagnards, or "mountaineers," were traditionally hostile to lowland Vietnamese, both Communist and noncommunist. The Hmong mountain people aided the Americans and became refugees after the war. Many built new lives in the United States.

Q What is a flash grenade and how is it used by the military?

A This device is like a hand grenade, but is non-lethal. The grenade's deafening bang and bright flash briefly confuse enemy troops, who then could be captured.

Q What nation has traditionally been Vietnam's worst oppressor?

A China: for 2,000 years, the Vietnamese struggled against Chinese rule. Their first rebellion was in 39AD, led by the legendary Truong sisters. The Chinese were driven out but reconquered Vietnam a few years later. Vietnam gained freedom again in 939AD.

Q Were the Vietnamese known historically as a warlike people?

A The Vietnamese battled five Chinese invasions after 939AD, becoming excellent warriors. They defeated the mighty conqueror Kublai Khan three times—the last in 1287, routing 300,000 Mongol invaders. China finally recognized Vietnam's independence in 1427.

Flash grenade

Q Where did Americans meet the fiercest fighting?

A The north, where South Vietnam bordered both North Vietnam and Laos. Fifty-three percent of Americans killed in Vietnam died in the four northernmost provinces: Quang Tri, Thua Thien, Quang Nam, and Quan Tin.

Q What was the prime air force target in North Vietnam?

A The 1.5-mile (2.3 km) Doumer Bridge, which carried the trains of four major railroad lines coming from the north into Hanoi. All freight moving by rail from China and from the seaport city of Haiphong crossed this important bridge, which also carried truck traffic.

K-9 unit soldier

Q Did South Vietnam's Buddhists demonstrate during the war?

A Yes, Buddhist monks regularly called for negotiations with the Communists. Priests praying in the streets for peace suffered oppression by government troops.

South Vietnamese Buddhist monks are penned in by barbed wire as they demonstrate in the early 1970s.

Timeline

In 1946, Vietnamese Communists and nationalists in eastern Indochina rose up against their French colonizers. This First Indochina War (1946–1954) ended with the defeat of the American-backed French. Vietnam was divided into the Communist North and capitalist South. For 20 more years, the United States supported South Vietnam, waging war against the Communists and nationalists. This Second Indochina War, known in the United States as the Vietnam War, cost the lives of more than 58,000 Americans, 1 million Vietnamese combatants, and 4 million Vietnamese civilians. In 1973, American troops withdrew from South Vietnam, which fell to the Communists two years later.

Destroyer USS *Maddox* in Gulf of Tonkin

1945–1946 INDOCHINA STRUGGLE
In August 1945, Japan surrenders to Allies in World War II (1939–1945) and gives up military control of French colonies in Indochina. Vietnamese Communist leader Ho Chi Minh declares the independent Democratic Republic of Vietnam (DRV). France sends troops to occupy Vietnam, sparking conflict; First Indochina War begins.

1950–1953 START OF U.S. ADVISORY PHASE
U.S. Military Assistance and Advisory Group (MAAG) is set up in 1950 to aid French against Vietminh, the rebel army. The United States supplies funding and military equipment to French forces. The insurgency strengthens and wins control of the countryside.

North Vietnamese stamp showing divided Vietnam

1954 TWO VIETNAMS
The fall in May 1954 of Dien Bien Phu, a major French base in northern Indochina, decisively ends the First Indochina War. Peace terms signed in Geneva, Switzerland, temporarily divide the country into the Vietminh-controlled DRV in the North and the Republic of Vietnam (RVN) in the South. Terms require that Vietnamese should vote on their form of government.

1955–1963 ARMED REVOLT
In 1955, Ngo Dinh Diem becomes president of South Vietnam. Backed by the United States, Diem refuses to allow a vote. Armed insurrection resumes, with the DRV supporting rebels known as Viet Cong (VC). U.S. military advisors increase to 16,000 by 1963, when the Army of the Republic of Vietnam (ARVN) is defeated at Ap Bac.

1963 ASSASSINATIONS
On November 2, an American-backed military coup in South Vietnam overthrows and assassinates Diem. U.S. president John F. Kennedy is assassinated on November 22; he is succeeded by Vice President Lyndon B. Johnson.

1964 GULF OF TONKIN INCIDENT
In August, the U.S. military alleges that North Vietnamese gunboats have attacked a U.S. vessel in the Gulf of Tonkin. The Senate passes Gulf of Tonkin Resolution giving Johnson broad war powers. Air strikes begin on North Vietnam.

1965 DIRECT U.S. INTERVENTION
February–March VC attack U.S. military base at Pleiku. In March, the first Marine combat troops are deployed to Vietnam, and the air campaign termed Operation Rolling Thunder begins. Johnson decides to increase U.S. forces in Vietnam to 33,000 troops.

June–July Battle at Dong Xoai pits U.S. Special Forces, sailors, and South Vietnamese troops against VC guerrillas. LBJ orders increase of U.S. forces to 125,000.

Green beret

August Operation Starlite, first major U.S. ground offensive; Operation Market Time attacks enemy seaborne supply routes to South Vietnam.

November Battle of Ia Drang Valley involves Air Cavalry assault, first major engagement by troops carried into battle and resupplied by helicopter. Pentagon calls for 400,000 troops.

1966 AIR AND GROUND WARFARE
January After a pause in bombing North Vietnam (in a failed attempt to begin negotiations) LBJ resumes air campaign.

March VC and North Vietnamese Army (NVA) troops attack and destroy U.S. Special Forces base in A Shau Valley.

June Massive U.S. air raids on Hanoi and the port city of Haiphong destroy much of North Vietnam's fuel supplies.

August Australian troops win Battle of Long Tan.

September–November Operation Attleboro drives VC forces across Cambodian border.

1967 WAR AND ANTIWAR
January Operation Bolo: air campaign inflicts heavy losses on North Vietnamese air force; in Operation Cedar Falls, U.S. and ARVN troops attack the VC-controlled "Iron Triangle" region near Saigon.

February In Operation Junction City, U.S. and ARVN strike enemy bases north of Saigon.

Peace-sign button

April Major antiwar demonstrations in New York City and San Francisco indicate U.S. public is not fully behind war.

Ngo Dinh Diem, front left, is welcomed at Washington National Airport by President Eisenhower, center, 1957.

May Defense Secretary Robert McNamara decides war policy is not working; recommends cutting back on bombing. LBJ troubled by doubt over right course to follow.

July Marines battle NVA at Con Thien; McNamara visits Saigon, agrees to add 55,000 more troops.

August The U.S. bombing campaign against North Vietnam intensifies.

October Huge antiwar march on Washington, D.C.; more than 50,000 protesters. Bombing of Hanoi/Haiphong increases.

November–December Battle of Dak To, a fierce clash between U.S. and NVA. McNamara resigns, objecting to bombing.

1968 DEPTHS OF WAR

January–February Massive NVA-VC offensive during the Buddhist New Year, called Tet. South Vietnam is aflame for weeks before the U.S. and government forces regain control.

ARVN troops recapture Citadel at Hué, during Tet Offensive.

January–April Siege of U.S. base at Khe Sanh; Marines fight off determined NVA attacks and hold out until siege is broken.

President Johnson consults with Secretary of Defense Robert McNamara in February 1968.

March My Lai Massacre: U.S. troops of the 23rd Infantry Division kill more than 300 civilians at the RVN hamlet of My Lai. Disheartened by growing opposition to the war, and his health failing, LBJ declares he will not run again for president.

July Phoenix program begins: secret campaign to kill enemy sympathizers allegedly kills 40,000 South Vietnamese.

October LBJ announces end to bombing campaign Rolling Thunder. During Rolling Thunder, more bombs were dropped on North Vietnam than the United States used in the Pacific Theater in World War II.

November Richard M. Nixon elected president, promising to bring peace with honor in Vietnam.

1969 PEACE DISCUSSIONS, WAR RAGES ON

January Preliminary meetings held in Paris for future peace talks. Marines conduct Operation Dewey Canyon, discovering network of enemy supply roads from Laos.

March Operation Menu: Nixon approves secret bombing campaign to strike enemy bases and supply routes in Cambodia. U.S. begins policy of "Vietnamization," meaning South Vietnamese take responsibility for their own defense.

May 101st Airborne troops capture Hill 937 in the "Battle of Hamburger Hill," costing 46 U.S. lives. Hill 937 is soon abandoned.

June Nixon announces that 25,000 troops will be withdrawn from Vietnam later in the year. Regular troop reductions will continue thereafter.

August U.S. secretary of state Henry Kissinger meets with North Vietnamese representative in Paris.

September Ho Chi Minh dies in Hanoi at the age of 79.

1970 WIDENING WAR

April–May U.S. troops invade Cambodia to attack Communist positions and bases.

May Ohio National Guard fires on antiwar demonstrators at Kent State University, killing four and wounding ten.

June Senate repeals Gulf of Tonkin Resolution that gave broad war powers to the president.

1971 VIETNAMIZATION AND WITHDRAWAL

February–April ARVN troops strike across Laotian border in Operation Lam Son.

November U.S. troops number only 139,000, down from a peak of 543,500 on April 30, 1969.

1972 BOMBS SPUR TALKS

February Nixon visits China, meets Mao Zedong and other leaders.

NVA attack in their 1972 offensive.

March–July NVA opens new offensives.

May–October In response to the NVA's offensives, Nixon orders Operation Linebacker, a massive bombing campaign against North Vietnam.

December Communist negotiators still hesitate to make peace, so Operation Linebacker II renews bombing, targets Hanoi and Haiphong.

1973–1975 COMMUNIST TRIUMPH

January 1973 Paris Peace Accords signed by U.S., North Vietnam, South Vietnam, and Viet Cong; U.S. military presence in Vietnam ends 60 days later.

August 1974 Nixon resigns in disgrace after the Watergate scandal threatens to bring his impeachment. Vice President Gerald R. Ford takes office, pardoning Nixon for any illegal acts he had committed.

January 1975 North Vietnam resumes military campaign to defeat South Vietnam.

March–April 1975 Final Communist offensive captures Saigon on April 30; North and South Vietnam are soon united as the Socialist Republic of Vietnam, with Hanoi as its capital.

U.S. troops board a helicopter to return home in 1969.

Find out more

THE STORY OF THE INDOCHINA CONFLICT is found at many museums, libraries, and Web sites, and at war memorials. The memorials are places where everyone can join in remembering and honoring those who served. Major memorials are in the United States, Vietnam, Australia, South Korea, and France—some have interactive displays and guided tours that bring the wartime experience to life.

VIETNAM

A national tribute

The Vietnam Veterans Memorial in Washington, D.C., honors Americans who served in the Vietnam War. "The Wall" is the central feature, engraved with the names of those who died. Two other components, added later, are the Three Servicemen statue and flagpole, and the Vietnam Women's Memorial. The national memorial, which takes no stand for or against the war, is one of the most visited U.S. monuments.

MEMORIAL IN AUSTRALIA
The Australian Vietnam Forces National Memorial, in the nation's capital, Canberra, was dedicated in October 1992. Its concrete forms are inspired by ancient sacred sites built of tall "standing stones." Soldiers' statements about the war are presented on an inside wall.

VIETNAM WOMEN'S MEMORIAL
This sculpture, by Glenna Goodacre, pays tribute to the women who served in Vietnam. Dedicated in November 1993, it shows three nurses with a wounded soldier. One nurse comforts him as another kneels in thought or prayer. The third nurse looks to the skies for help—perhaps from a medevac helicopter or from a higher power.

THREE SERVICEMEN
Fredrick Hart designed this memorial, which portrays soldiers in the field. It was dedicated in the fall of 1984.

TAKING A RUBBING
Visitors to The Wall can place paper against an engraved name and rub with a pencil to create a copy. The National Park Service conducts ceremonies at the site on Memorial Day and Veterans Day.

THE WALL OF NAMES
A line of visitors forms under rainy skies at the Vietnam memorial in Washington, D.C., in November 2004. This polished granite wall, designed by architect Maya Lin, holds the names of more than 58,200 U.S. dead and missing. Dedicated in November 1982, the $8.4 million memorial was established by the Vietnam Veterans Memorial Fund, founded by Vietnam veterans.

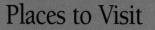

NATIONAL MUSEUM OF AMERICAN HISTORY, WASHINGTON, D.C.
Smithsonian's "The Price of Freedom: Americans At War" exhibit examines the ways war has shaped American history, and also features a display dedicated to the Vietnam War.

NATIONAL MUSEUM OF THE U.S. AIR FORCE, DAYTON, OHIO
Visit the largest military aviation museum in the world. Featured are exhibits of U.S. helicopters and fixed-wing aircraft of the Vietnam War.

NEW YORK VIETNAM VETERANS MEMORIAL, NEW YORK CITY
Excerpts of letters, diary entries, and poems written by Americans during the Vietnam era are etched into the New York Vietnam Veterans Memorial wall. These personal writings are supplemented by news dispatches and public statements.

VIETNAM-ERA EDUCATION CENTER, NEW JERSEY VIETNAM VETERANS' MEMORIAL, HOLMDEL, NEW JERSEY
The first museum of its kind in the United States, the center is dedicated solely to the Vietnam War. The collection includes photographs, historic timelines, films, interactive displays, personal letters, and more.

THE IMPERIAL CITADEL, HUÉ, VIETNAM
The Citadel, in Hué, was the residence of the Nguyen emperors. Hué was Vietnam's imperial capital from 1804 through 1945. Much of the Citadel was reduced to rubble during the Tet Offensive of 1968. The old fort and imperial structures are gradually being restored.

THE WEST POINT MUSEUM, WEST POINT, NEW YORK
The galleries of the West Point Museum interpret the history of the U.S. Army from colonial times to the present. Weapons, uniforms, and art are featured in displays devoted to the Vietnam conflict. An NVA uniform is shown along with the muddy jungle fatigues of the American infantryman in Vietnam.

MEMORIAL IN FRANCE
The Memorial to the Wars in Indochina honors veterans of France's Indochina wars. Near Fréjus in southeastern France, the memorial was inaugurated in 1993. It holds the remains of more than 23,000 French—including 3,515 civilians—who died between 1940 and 1954. An educational room tells about France's century-long Indochina wars.

AUSTRALIA'S WAR MUSEUM
The Australian War Memorial is a museum that honors the dead from all the nation's wars. Located near Canberra, it is a place where loved ones can grieve. Also, the museum teaches understanding of war itself through exhibits and research facilities.

TUNNEL TOURS
The former VC tunnel complex at Cu Chi is one of Vietnam's most popular tourist attractions. The visitors' center displays diagrams showing how the tunnels were used. Tours take visitors into the tunnels to see reconstructed living spaces, including barracks, meeting rooms, and kitchens.

USEFUL WEB SITES

- Comprehensive online research site, created in association with The Vietnam Project at Texas Tech University:
  star.vietnam.ttu.edu/index.htm
- Photographs from a North Vietnamese perspective:
  www.anothervietnam.com
- National Park Service site with an in-depth history of the making of the Vietnam Veterans Memorial:
  www.nps.gov/vive
- Visitors can use online technology to locate specific names and personal information of service members on The Wall:
  www.viewthewall.com
- An online museum of Vietnam War-era artifacts and other memorabilia:
  www.vietnamwall.org
- Great photographs and general information about the Vietnam War:
  www.vietnampix.com
- More about the Mobile Riverine Force, and war on Vietnam's waterways:
  www.mrfa.org

LEARNING ABOUT THE WAR
Vietnamese schoolchildren take a class trip to view a MiG-21 fighter at a Hanoi military museum in 2000. This plane was in the squadron that defended their city against U.S. air raids. The trip is part of Vietnam's 25th-anniversary celebration of the April 30, 1975, fall of Saigon.

Glossary

AGENT ORANGE Toxic chemical used by American military to kill vegetation and thus deprive the enemy of food and hiding places in the jungle. Sprayed from aircraft and by hand. Many Vietnam veterans and Vietnamese suffer health problems caused by inhaling Agent Orange. Its name came from the orange stripe that identified its steel-drum containers.

AIRBORNE Soldiers who are trained parachutists, also called paratroopers. In Vietnam, these troops usually went into action on helicopters that carried them to battle.

AIR CAVALRY Nicknamed "Air Cav," these are helicopter-borne infantry who were supported by fire from helicopter gunships; many Air Cav troopers were members of former horse cavalry regiments.

AIRMOBILE Helicopter-borne (heliborne) infantry, such as Air Cav, whose units and tactics were first developed during the Vietnam War.

AK–47 assault rifle

AK-47 Soviet-manufactured Kalashnikov assault rifle that was a favored weapon of the VC and NVA.

APC Armored personnel carrier—an armor-plated vehicle used for transporting troops or supplies; usually armed with a .50-caliber heavy machine gun.

ARVIN Nickname for South Vietnamese soldiers in the Army of the Republic of (South) Vietnam.

ARVN Acronym for the Army of the Republic of (South) Vietnam: the South Vietnamese regular army.

BASE CAMP A central resupply base for units in the field; location for command headquarters, artillery batteries, and airfields.

BIRD Soldiers' term for a helicopter or any aircraft.

BOAT PEOPLE South Vietnamese refugees who fled by boat after the Communist victory in 1975. Boatloads of desperate refugees sailed across the South China Sea, and thousands drowned. Many were rescued and taken in by neighboring countries and the United States.

BODY COUNT The military's count of the number of enemy troops that had been killed during an operation.

CHARLIE Nickname for Viet Cong or NVA; taken from "Victor Charlie," the military radioman's code for the letters *V* and *C* in messages about Viet Cong, or VC.

CHINOOK CH-47 cargo helicopter used to supply American and Allied troops.

CHOPPER A helicopter; Vietnam was the first "helicopter war" because it saw the first major use of rotary-wing aircraft for transportation of troops during military campaigns.

CLAYMORE Widely used antipersonnel mine that, when detonated, hurled small projectiles up to 300 feet (100 m).

COBRA AH-1G attack helicopter, armed with rockets and machine guns.

COMPOUND A fortified U.S. or Allied installation that served as a camp and fortress.

CONCERTINA WIRE Coiled barbed wire with razor-sharp edges that was laid to protect the outer perimeter of a fortified position. Enemy troops would have to cut this wire before they could break through and attack.

COUNTERINSURGENCY Organized antiguerrilla (anti-insurgent) warfare that armed and trained local militias to defend their communities against the enemy. Counterinsurgency methods included using guerrilla tactics of surprise, concealment, and assassination to strike at enemy guerrillas.

C-rations

C-RATIONS Combat rations, or meals, for use in the field; each meal usually included a canned main course and fruit, packets of dessert, powdered cocoa, sugar, cream, and coffee; there was also a pack of cigarettes and some chewing gum.

DEFOLIATION The process of destroying vegetation (foliage) usually by spraying toxic chemicals such as Agent Orange, widely used in Vietnam.

DMZ The Demilitarized Zone that was the dividing line between North and South Vietnam at the 17th parallel. The DMZ was established in 1954 under the Geneva Accords. It was to be kept free of any military installations or occupation.

DRV Democratic Republic of Vietnam— the original name given by Ho Chi Minh to Vietnam when he proclaimed independence from France in 1945. When Vietnam was divided in 1954, the name referred only to Communist-dominated North Vietnam, with the capital Hanoi.

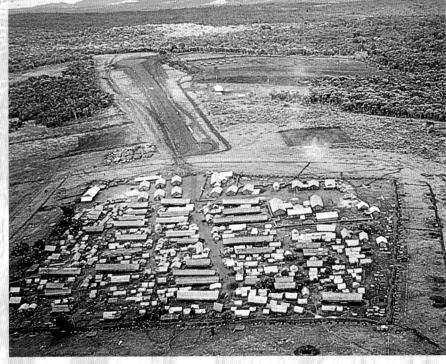

Special Forces base camp in the Central Highlands

DUSTOFF Emergency evacuation of the wounded by medical helicopter; a medevac.

Dustoff buckle

FIRE BASE A temporary artillery encampment, or compound, set up to support nearby ground operations with cannon fire or rockets.

FIREFIGHT A brief battle, or exchange of small-arms fire, with the enemy.

FLAK JACKET A fiberglass-filled vest worn for protection from shrapnel—small pieces of metal hurled by the explosion of shells, mines, or grenades.

FRIENDLY FIRE Accidental attacks on U.S. or Allied soldiers by other U.S. or Allied soldiers, aircraft, or artillery—usually the result of being mistaken for the enemy.

Flak jacket

GREEN BERETS U.S. Special Forces trained in counterinsurgency warfare and for operations behind enemy positions; they wore green berets.

GRUNT U.S. infantry's humorous term for infantryman—the lowest in military status.

GUNSHIP An armed helicopter or fixed-wing aircraft used to support ground troops and to patrol in search of enemy activity.

HAMMER AND ANVIL Tactic of partially encircling an enemy position with one force while other units drive the enemy out of hiding. The first force is the anvil, and the second is the hammer that attempts to smash the enemy against that anvil.

HANOI HILTON Nickname of North Vietnam's Hoa Lo Prison given by Americans held prisoner there; Hiltons are famous luxury hotels found around the world.

HUEY Nickname for the UH-1 series of helicopters, which were used for many purposes during the war.

IN-COUNTRY A soldier serving in Vietnam was said to be "in-country."

IRON TRIANGLE Viet Cong-dominated area, mainly jungle and rice paddies, between the Thi Tinh and Saigon rivers northwest of Saigon.

LZ A landing zone, usually a small protected clearing near the battlefront for the landing of resupply helicopters. LZs often grew to become permanent base camps interrupting enemy supply lines or troop movements.

MAAG Military Assistance and Advisory Group; U.S. headquarters formed in 1950 to aid the French military effort in Indochina.

MACV Military Assistance Command, Vietnam; headquarters that replaced MAAG in 1962; had overall command of U.S. forces in Vietnam until 1973.

MEDEVAC Evacuation of the wounded from the battlefield by helicopter.

MIA "Missing in Action," the military term for a serviceman or woman whose whereabouts after combat is not known.

M-16 American assault rifle used by U.S. and ARVN troops and many Allies.

NAM U.S. and Allied soldiers' nickname for Vietnam.

NAPALM A jellied petroleum material which burns fiercely; fired from flamethrowers or contained in bombs that explode and spread flaming jelly.

NLF National Liberation Front, the political wing of the South Vietnamese insurgency fighting against the Republic of (South) Vietnam.

NVA North Vietnamese Army, the regular troops of the Democratic Republic of (North) Vietnam.

POW "Prisoner of War," a serviceman or woman who has been captured by the enemy; POWs have specific rights in accordance with the laws of war that have been accepted by most nations.

PUNJI STICKS Sharpened bamboo stakes set in camouflaged pits, or mantraps; punjis pierce the bodies of those who fall into the pit.

RANGERS Elite commandos in the U.S. Army, specially trained for long-range reconnaissance (scouting) and dangerous combat missions.

RVN Republic of Vietnam, the official name given to South Vietnam when established in 1954 by its first president, Ngo Dinh Diem. The RVN capital was Saigon, the largest city in the South.

SEABEES Navy construction engineers famous for their ability to construct airfields, bases, and roads swiftly, often under combat conditions. Derived from the letters *CB* for "construction battalion."

SEALS Navy personnel who are members of special warfare "Sea, Air, Land" teams.

SEARCH AND DESTROY Operations in which troops searched an area in order to locate and destroy Communist forces; this often also included destroying supply caches and living quarters.

STRATEGIC HAMLETS Fortified villages, often in isolated farming areas, set up by U.S. and ARVN forces to protect the people against attacks or threats from Communist insurgents. Local militia were trained to defend these compounds.

TET The Buddhist lunar New Year. Thousands of Viet Cong guerrillas attacked U.S. and ARVN positions during the celebration of the Tet holiday in 1968.

TUNNEL RATS Originally termed "tunnel runners," the men who crawled into VC tunnels later took this nickname.

Tunnel rat gas mask

VC Short for Viet Cong, which in turn is the Vietnamese nickname for South Vietnamese Communist guerrillas operating in South Vietnam.

VIETNAMESE POPULAR FORCES South Vietnamese local military units, usually militia forces made up of civilians rather than regular soldiers.

VIETNAMIZATION U.S. policy to turn over the fighting to the South Vietnamese Army; this policy was established by President Richard M. Nixon late in the war, during the withdrawal of American troops.

ZIPPO A flamethrower that shot out flaming napalm; named after a type of cigarette lighter. A "Zippo" was also a gunboat armed with a flamethrower, and the phrase "Zippo job" referred to a mission to set Communist-held villages or positions on fire.

Zippo in a firefight

Index

Acknowledgments

DK Publishing, Inc. and Media Projects Inc., offer grateful thanks to: Clifford J. Rogers, Associate Professor of History, United States Military Academy; Steve R. Waddell, Associate Professor of History, United States Military Academy; Erika Rubel; Mark Tolf; David Mager; Michael Harris; Albert Moore; Doug Niven; Tim Page; Emma Naidoo; Jim Messinger; Bob Taylor; Justin Saffell; Ed Emering; Robert W. King; Ngo Vinh Long; Rev. Diedrik Nelson; Margie Ortiz and Terry Adams; Sema at Art-Hanoi; Ronnie Oldham; Jeff Lindsay; Tex Pantaleo; Robert H. Stoner, USNR (Ret.); Ron Toelke for cartography; Rob Stokes for relief mapping; Brian A. Benedict; Madeline Mancini; and Madeline Farbman.

Photography and Art Credits
(t=top; b=bottom; l=left; r=right; c=center; a=above)
American Museum of Military History: 33bl. **joelscoins.com:** 7tl. **anothervietnam.com:** © Mai Nam, 21brc; © Tran Phac, 22tl; © Le Minh Truong, 22–23, 23cr, 25b, 40–41; © Vo Anh Khanh, 33br; © VNA, 44bl, 56–57tc; © Duong Thanh Phong, 46tl, 60–61. **Art-hanoi.com:** 4crt, 19bc. **Associated Press:** 10bl, 13br, 38–39c, 69tl. **Australian War Memorial:** 69tcl. **Bernie Boston:** 50bl. **Boston University Archives:** 39tr. **brownwater-navy.com:** 42cr. **James Burmester:** 4clt, 15bc, 37br, 53cr. **Michael Burr:** 19r, 19bc. **Canadian Forces National Defense Ministry:** 4crb, 63cl. **CORBIS:** 35cr, 58bl; © Alinari

Archives/CORBIS: 7tr; Bettman/CORBIS: 6cl; 7cr, 8tl, 8tr, 8–9b, 9cl, 9bc, 10tr, 10c, 16bc, 17c, 17br, 18b, 20br, 21br, 25tl, 31c, 34bl, 34–35tc, 38tl, 38bl, 38bc, 39cl, 39crt, 40b, 42bl, 43tr, 43cr, 45br, 50cl, 50–51ca, 51tl, 51tr, 51cr, 51bl, 53bl, 54–55, 55tr, 57tr, 57bl, 60bc, 60bl, 63tr; © George Hall/CORBIS: 34br; © Jeremy Horner/CORBIS: 62tl; © Hulton-Deutsch Collection/CORBIS: 21t; © John R. Jones, Papilio/CORBIS: 46cr, 69bcl; © Catherine Karnow/CORBIS: 64bl; © Wally McNamee/CORBIS: 63cr; © Francoise de Mulder/CORBIS: 61tr; © Tim Page/CORBIS: 38cl, 62–63bc; © Steve Raymer/CORBIS: 63b; Reuters/CORBIS: 69bl; © Roman Soumar/CORBIS: 46br; CORBIS SYGMA: 6tr; © Darren Whiteside/Reuters/CORBIS: 62bl. **DK Picture Library:** © DK Picture Library: 48tl; © DK Picture Library, courtesy Museum of American Politcal Life/University of Hartford: 51br (inset); © Philip Blenkinsop/DK Picture Library: 70–71 bkgnd; © DK Picture Library, courtesy of Andrew L. Chernack: 23cl, 26b (scarf, canteen, pouch, oil can), 28cc (NVA knife); © David Mager/DK Picture Library, courtesy Mark Tolf: 2cr, 4tr, 4tc, 4bl, 11cl, 13cl, 15tr (inset), 27 lower cr, 27 upper c, 27tr, 29t (M-1 carbine, access.), 29cl (cleaning kit and grenades), 29c (M16 access.), 30bl, 30tl (inset), 30cl, 31tl, 31tr (inset), 32cl, 32bc, 33cl, 35tr (patches), 37bc, 38tr, 41c (inset), 47 (all equipment), 49tr, 51cr (inset), 55bl, 56cl (medal), 58bc, 65bl, 66cr, 70tr, 71r; © Stephen Oliver/DK Picture Library: 11bc; © Tim Ridley/DK Picture Library, courtesy of

the Ministry of Defence Pattern Room, Nottingham: 2tcl, 28bcl (RPG-7 and accessories), 29tcr (M16A1), 29bcr (M79); © Laura Wickenden/DK Picture Library: 46bcl. **Emering Coll.:** 2tr, 9bl (inset), 14tr, 15c (inset), 20tl, 37tc, 37te, 37tcr, 37cr, 37b, 59tc (POW & medal), 61cr, 62cr. **Folio, Inc.** © Rob Crandall: 68cl. **Michael Harris:** 62cl. **Lyndon Baines Johnson Pres. Lib.:** 11br, 15t, 20tl, 24tl, 48cl, 67cl. **John F. Kennedy Pres. Lib.:** 11tr. **Robert W. King:** 21tr (inset). **Coll. Ted Laurenson/©Diggitt McLaughlin:** 4tl, 16tl, 17cl, 50tr, 66br. **LJMilitaria:** 20bc (inset), 55tc, 56cl, 56cl (patch). **John P. Conway/ vhpamuseum.org:** 32tl, 55cr, 71tl. **Library of Congress:** 10–11c, 11cr, 13tr, 14c, 14b, 16br, 16–17b, 17tl, 18cl, 19b, 21cl, 21bl, 23tc, 24b, 24cl, 26cl, 32cl, 39br, 45tc, 45cl, 45cr, 47tl, 47br, 49tr, 50tr, 52tr, 53cr, 53tl, 54cl, 55br, 57tc, 57br, 59tr, 60tl, 60cl (UPI), 61br, 66bc. © **Jeff Lindsay:** 65tl. **Mobile Riverine Forces Association/© Dan Dodd:** 34cl, 42c (two patches, inset), 42cr, 43tl, 71b. **MPI Archives:** 2c, 50t, 50tc, 59br, 65b. **Andrea Morland:** 68tr. **National Archives:** 2br, 6bl, 8bl, 9tc, 12cl, 14tl, 14tcl, 15cr, 15bl, 16tc, 16tr, 16bl, 16–17b, 17tr, 18tl, 19cl, 23tr, 23br, 24tr, 25tr, 25cr, 26–27cr, 27tl, 27bl, 27ccr, 28tl, 28tr, 28br, 28cl (grenades), 29br, 32tr, 32bl, 33bc, 33tr, 35b, 36bl, 36–37, 37tl, 39tc, 40c, 41tr, 41cr, 41tr, 43tr, 44tr, 44cr, 44cl, 45tr, 46tcl, 46bl, 49cr, 52b, 65tr, 66–67 bkgnd, 67b, 70br. NPS/Terry Allen: 68b, 68–69 bkgnd. **National Vietnam War Museum:** 34c (inset). Naval Hist. Soc.: 12cr.

12–13c. Rev. Diedrik Nelson: 4clb, 9r, 56cl. **Ronnie Max Oldham:** 14cl. **Ngo Vinh Long:** 7cl, 23bc. **Stars and Stripes:** 39tl. **Texas Tech:** 25cl (inset), 29bl, 64tc, 64tr, 67tl, 70l; Anonymous Coll.: 58–59tc, 63tl, 64br; Peter Braestrup Coll.: 49br; Donald Jellema Coll.: 2tl, 28clt, 28bcr, 31cl, 31b, 56br, 64br, 67tr; Douglas Pike Coll.: 13tl, 15cl, 39cr (Cronkite), 48bl, 48cr, 54bl, 56bl; Brig. Gen. Edwin H. Simmons Coll.: 48–49bc. **Tim Page:** 1, 3, 15br, 30tl, 30–31, 31tr, 44–45b, 56bl, 56br, 62t. **Theodore Schweitzer III:** 58cl. **Tribune Media Service:** 38cr. **U.S. Air Force:** 20cl, 21tcr, 34tl, 36tl, 36tr. **U.S. Army:** 17tr, 27crb, 49tl, 52cl, 55tl, 56–57cc. **U.S. Army Ctr for Mil. Hist.:** 6–7bc, 11tl, 52tr (inset), 65tl. **U.S. Army Mil. Hist. Inst.:** 65cr. **U.S. Navy:** 12bl, 42tr, 43cl, 58bc (nurse). **U.S. Navy, Naval Hist. Ctr:** 2 clb, 12c (inset), 12–13b, 66rr. **Vietnam Veterans Assoc. of Australia:** 63tr. **VietnamWall.org:** 2bl, 2bc, 9tl (inset), 10cl, 25tl (patch), 26ct, 27br, 28bl, 30c, 33cr, 58tl, 58tc (bracelet), 64tl, 65tl (bracelet & flute); 71cl.

Cover Credits:
Bettman/CORBIS: front b, back b; **DK Picture Library:** © DK Picture Library: front tl (sandal & helmet), front tr; © DK Picture Library, courtesy of Andrew L. Chernack: back tc, back c; © Tim Ridley/DK Picture Library, courtesy of the Ministry of Defence Pattern Room, Nottingham: back cl; **National Archives:** front (mine); **U.S. Army Ctr. for Mil. Hist.:** front tc (flag), front tlc (medals); VietnamWall.org: back cr, back tl.